Words from the Maestro

JOYCE H. HYNES

Words from the Maestro

The Reading Glass Books
(888) 420-3050
www.readingglassbooks.com
fulfillment@readingglassbooks.com

Words from the Maestro

Pitch
Introduction

Faith, love, music and laughter is the theme of *"Whispers of Music."*

Set in Putnum County, WV., a prestigious music school prepares to hold auditions for second semester classes.

The director, cancerous and rude prefers to watch TV sports to auditioning the twenty-six students over the three-day session. The Director's heart is changed by two unsuspecting characters and one strange phenomenon.

Feel the Love of God as you read, venture deep into the holler of the mountains, enjoy laughter with the clowns, and listen for a whisper from the Master's.

P.S. Did I mention the 26 students are animals with matching instruments according to their alphabetical namesake. Enjoy Director Ensemble Elk as he takes you thru the alphabet of music.

Composition of Life

Compose yourself a melody of life,
Tune into your feelings.
Stay sharp; don't go flat!
Don't fret the small steps of the day.
Waltz through your day with a signature smile.
Look at life's many arrangements.
Live in harmony; keep your tempo uplifting.
Fill the lines and spaces of your life with laughter.
Stand up and take note of all your blessings.
Any step you take whether quarter, half or whole,
Is a measure of success that makes up the phrases of life.
Whistle when feeling down and out.
Singing will refresh your heart, mind and soul.
Keep and song in your heart at all times.
Correct any discords before the sun sets.
Accentuate the good times,
Don't let the hurdles of the day diminish your self-worth.
Every day has different rhythms,
Enjoy each one that comes your way.
The melody of life consists of peace, patience, love, kindness,
Understanding and forgiveness.

©1999Joyce H. Hynes

Chapter 1
Director Ensemble

Director Ensemble is asleep in his office chair at Abington Academy. Persistent snoring causes the white ruffling to unfurl to the floor. What were once vibrant red curtains now hang dully, and the windows are missing their glass. With a sudden snort, he awakens.

He struggles to sit upright as he swings his legs over the top of yesterday's mail. He briefly glances at it, brushing half the pile to the floor. On top of the desk, an envelope hauntingly looks back. This is not the first envelope he has received. For several months, Director Ensemble has played kick the mail under the rug or file it in a location that is "gone" but not lost.

Plenty of loose ends need to be tidied up or delegated before the second semester begins tomorrow at Abington

1

Academy. Paper and pencil in hand, Director Ensemble begins noting his thoughts on his new handheld computer, which he ordered off the internet. Supplies need to be purchased, and budgets need to be secured. Because of the recent COVID event, the academy requires certain upgrades, along with new health regulations. Rosters for private lessons, practice room scheduling, and orchestral instrument rentals will need special attention because of the outbreak. So much to do in a whisper of time.

"Ms. Treble Clef Catbird, where's my coffee? I can't think without my go-to juice," he calls out and then mutters to himself, "Guess she and I need a little talk. Our discussions have gone by the wayside and need to be reinstated. Where are you? Must I get my coffee myself?"

Ms. Treble Clef, one of the director's secretaries, comes barreling in with a smile the size of Texas. A chirpy bird, she is anxious to organize, arrange, and assist him with anything in any size, shape, or form. He constantly needs work-related reminders but never forgets to rearrange the tuft of feathers on top of her head. Today, he adds two more assignments: cleanup and curtain duty.

"Ms. Treble Clef, you're three minutes late! You know I need coffee first thing in the morning. I'm old and need fossil fuel! Time is valued at Abington!"

"Yes, sir! Coming right up!"

* * *

In the kitchen, she examines the recent remodeling. Narrow and compact, the kitchen is well organized. White cabinets of various sizes line one wall, and small appliances are on the other. A farm-style sink is underneath, with two crystal lights that highlight the butcher-block countertops. Ms. Treble Clef knows how to fix his coffee. Good thing or she might end up wearing it! Special coffee and special cup for Director Ensemble. She cannot figure out why he won't fix it himself.

"Before you get settled and comfy, please don't forget tomorrow's the big day. Or has that skipped your mind?" he says when she brings the coffee back in.

"Sir, how could I possibly forget? Can't we afford a cleaning service? Those carpenters failed to clean and empty their trash before they walked at quitting time. Can't we afford a cleaning service like Kwick Klean? I hear they're very thorough and reasonable. My secretarial duties are expanding, and I'll never catch-up doing coffee duty."

Her answer is a grunt from Director Ensemble, meaning, "No!" Frustrated, Ms. Treble Clef goes to the utility room to prepare a bucket of warm water with cleaning solution. After walking over to the left corner, she struggles to get down on her skinny little chicken knees and then begins to swab the floor like a sailor. Pain wobbles all the way from her pitiful legs to the end of her beak, but she continues.

Director Ensemble comes into the kitchen and watches for a moment. Then he jibber-jabbers, feeling no guilt, and leaves her to complete the duties. Before venturing back to his office to watch TV, he delegates even more duties to Ms. Treble Clef.

She mumbles, "Can't afford a cleaning lady? Well, that's a bunch of horse feathers, sir! Ouch! That smarts. Where's my little kneepads?"

Ms. Treble Clef continues cleaning until everything is pick 'n' clean, just like on Thanksgiving when the wishbone is clean as a whistle and dry as a bone. "Oh, my little knees! I just scraped some of the skin off," she says, rubbing her knee.

From his office, Director Ensemble bellows, "Ms. Treble Clef, have you lost your mind, or did you leave it with those knee things? My hands are empty, my mouth is dry, and you must be brainless, bird! I've been working, and my mouth is a desert. Get up, and bring me some coffee!"

"Don't you mean hardly working, sir? Oh, I'll go and get more of your precious coffee, but next time, get it yourself, sir!" One last time, Ms. Treble Clef fixes his coffee. She plans a special treat of crackers and peanut butter, hoping it will stick to the roof of his mouth to shut him up! Round crackers with two tablespoons of peanut butter should do the trick—or at least lower the volume so she can complete the final preparations for tomorrow.

Tray in hand, she knocks and waits for a response. After three times, she enters, finding him glued to the TV, watching baseball and unaware of her presence. "Sir, your snack."

"Are you talking to me? Can't you see I'm involved here?"

Ms. Treble Clef quietly backs away, catching sight of an envelope marked *Urgent*. Her beady eyes want a closer look, but the wall clock rings in unison with the rumbling of her stomach. She hates the thought of disturbing the director again but knows it's her duty. "Sir, it's time for my lunch break. I'm going to the Perfect Pitch Café and will return soon."

The Perfect Pitch Café is a five-minute walk from Abington Academy. Ms. Treble Clef is so relieved to be away from Director Ensemble her feathers puff outward from relaxation. During her break, the "call" of the envelope in his office won't leave her alone. Nothing urgent has happened in this school the entire twenty years she'd been employed. Everything is so laid back even a tortoise moves faster. However, tomorrow this will all change.

The Jason Mixolydian School of Music will premiere on the campus of Abington Academy during the second semester. In addition to orientation, the students will have an assessment of their musical knowledge and performance skills. Classmates will participate in a concert scheduled at a later date.

Enrollment has been slowly declining the last few years, and Director Ensemble hopes that with the addition of the Jason Mixolydian group, the remodeling, and electronic upgrades, the school will once again be the premier place to study music.

Director Ensemble intently watches football while eating the peanut butter crackers prepared by Ms. Treble Clef. One by one, he listens as the crunchiness of the crackers resonates in his head. The sound of his teeth blasts through the crackers like dynamite exploding off a mountaintop. A sensory symphony fills each cell with energy. The peanut butter is thick and mixes with his saliva until a gooey wad fills his oral cavity. He desperately needs a drink, but whom is he to call? His cup is empty and requires him to get up! Now what? He convinces himself to walk down to the galley. Having sat so long, his body has molded to the chair and now he's stuck! Ensemble wiggles until his body releases from the suction grip. Standing, he ventures down to the galley in search of something wet.

Rummaging through several cabinets, he finds a paper cup for water. Over at the sink, he fills a glass to release the sticky peanut butter's mighty grip from the roof of his mouth. Several swallows, and down it goes. Now he's free to yell at whomever he wants, but nobody's home. He refills his cup a second time and clears his mouth completely.

Director Ensemble returns to his desk, where he sits, motionless. He picks up the large envelope and stares at it. The sticker on the front says "*Open at Once.*" There is no need to open or read it because he already knows the contents: another foreclosure note related to the academy. He's lost count of the actual number of notices he's received.

Somehow, the envelope draws him in, despite the problems at the academy. The envelope keeps beckoning. Finally, he decides to open it. Maybe it's not a foreclosure note, even though it's from Signature Financial.

Director Ensemble reaches for the letter opener and feels anger. He throws the opener across the room with such force it pierces the wall. Furious with himself, he tosses the envelope aside and then steps outside and walks to the pond.

The water has a hypnotic effect. He feels calmer. Scanning the water, he sees small ripples surface. A flutter piques his curiosity, and he searches for the source. Carefully, he approaches the water. He is shocked to discover two clownfish setting up housekeeping at the far end. Bending down, he's surprised when one pops up:

"Hi! My name is Ding."

Then another says, "Hello! I'm Dong. We are the Doorbells! Want to hear our ringtones?"

In a flash, they return to the water, only a wave marking their position. Director Ensemble is unsure what just happened. Walking back to the academy, he cannot stop thinking about the two aquatic creatures. *Ding was purple. Clownfish aren't supposed to be purple; orange and white are their natural colors. This one was entirely purple—hair, fins, and those lips! How in the world did it get that way?* The other one looked somewhat normal; its colors were those of a clownfish, but its laugh would shatter his coffee cup to pieces.

Back at his desk, he sits in silence. He thinks about returning to the sports channel, but the calling of the envelope is too strong. Stowed under the carpet for safekeeping with the edge sticking out, the envelope is clearly visible. He picks the envelope off the floor with his long, hairy right arm. Holding it up to the light, Director Ensemble takes a sneak peek at what's inside. Much to his dismay, he is only able to decipher the heading, *Signature Financial.*

Grasping the envelope between thumb and index finger, he searches the perimeters for a clue. The paper-thin contents give Director Ensemble no details. Disappointed, he thrusts the envelope back under the rug.

His stomach ignites a growl as big as an elephant's, indicating it's time for supper. He calls for Ms. Treble Clef for takeout. No response. He walks to the lobby and finds a note stating she has gone for the night and will return in the morning to prepare for the influx of students. Director Ensemble locks up for the evening and walks the short distance home, unable to forget the two clownfish.

Chapter 2

Ms. Treble Clef, Secretary

A vivid-blue, cloudless morning in the West Virginia mountains welcomes a special day. Ms. Treble Clef awakens, realizing she's overslept. Falling out of bed, she trips over

Staccato, her orange-and-cream-colored tabby cat. Staccato gives her a sharp right claw for the disturbance.

Ms. Treble Clef hurriedly dabs on her morning face. Disregarding the electric curlers, she pulls back her long locks using scrunchies, forgetting several gray tufts on top of her pointed head. Her right wing travels over all the clothes hanging in the closet as she searches for today's look. Stopping at a black skirt and crisp white blouse, she pulls the garments from the fabric hangers. Her body stiffens in shock as she finds that tic-tac-toe has been played on her skirt and blouse in red ink.

"I can't go to work like this! I must make another selection. Director Ensemble will pluck my feathers one by one for coming in wearing a gaming outfit! Today of all days! Students will be selected for the musical event of the year. I've got to look my catbird best." She sighs, putting the clothes aside. "Jeepers, I wish I'd done my laundry."

The letters "GDPYT" appear on the fogged mirror in the bathroom. Ms. Treble Clef tries to think of a song with those letters in the title. She taps her beak, naming several songs. She's been state winner three years running for "Name That Tune," as past and present songs constantly play in her head. However, this time, she's unable to identify one with the letters GDPYT.

A voice within speaks: "Stop, Treble! Focus, and put your tufted head on straight before you lay an egg! *Get dressed! Pull yourself together!*" That's it! Excitement overwhelms Ms. Treble Clef. She returns to the closet and picks another outfit for the day: navy-blue bell-bottom pants and a cream-colored blouse. After teasing hair tufts, she peeks in the mirror.

A voice speaks: "Whoa, Treble! You'll never get to work at this rate. Get on your hoverboard and move!" Since the hoverboard is unavailable, she grabs her purse, locks the front door, and then heads for the car. After she turns the ignition key, the engine purrs like a kitten during a good belly rub. Ms. Treble Clef's mind races, knowing preparations need attention before the students arrive.

The crisp mountain air revives her spirit. She's ready to face Director Ensemble. *I really need to be early. So much to do in a whisper of time*, she thinks.

Arriving at the academy, Ms. Treble Clef takes a big breath and then gingerly walks through the front door, wearing the big smile of a clown minus the red nose. Her heart races in anticipation of arriving students. They soak up each note of music like a sponge and appreciate every minute of instruction. *They pick you up when you're feeling down; music is wonderful medicine.*

After looking at the office clock, she starts typing the daily schedule. There's a loud noise. Director Ensemble hoofs through the front door, yelling, "Coffee! Coffee! Where's my coffee? Bring me my special cup! My nerves are shot. How many students, Ms. Treble Clef? How many?"

Ms. Treble Clef pleasantly replies, "Nine, sir. This morning, we have nine."

She scurries to fix his coffee but spills the entire pot on the floor. She frantically begins wiping it up. "Oh, brother! Better fix another pot lickety-split!"

A few minutes later, coffee in hand, she knocks on the office door of Director Ensemble. "Knock, knock, sir! It's me."

"I know who it is. Come in, and put the coffee on the table. Tell me when one comes."

"One what, sir?"

"Student, birdbrain! Are we expecting Santa Claus or the Easter Bunny?"

Ms. Treble Clef cautiously sets the coffee down. "Your coffee, sir." Curious as a cat, she wonders what has flustered the director to this grade of agitation.

She empties the trash full of soda bottles and candy bar wrappers as her eyes wander, looking for the envelope she saw before. Alas, she locates it and squints to see the addressee, but only the word *urgent* is clear.

"Ms. Treble Clef, do you need something? Did you lose your earring back?" "Sir, I wasn't snooping. I have something in my eye!"

"Yeah, right! Get out of my sight!"

Ms. Treble Clef shuts the director's door and returns to the reception desk, leaving the director alone, looking out the large window. He is compelled to take a closer look. Out on the pond, a strange phenomenon is taking place: bubbles! Bubbles are magically floating on top of the water! Initially motionless, they are now rising slowly, capturing the attention of Director Ensemble. He goes outside to look. A wave appears—not a water wave but one from a clownfish. Two exposed eyes break the surface only to vanish in the wink of an eye. Director Ensemble walks back to the academy, puzzled.

Ms. Treble Clef's whiskers twitch in anticipation of students with specialty instruments arriving from other countries. She knows her mind is not entirely focused, having seen a part of the envelope marked "Urgent." *Not that again!* The catchy little phrase or song lyric that constantly plays in your head, also known as the Song Stuck Syndrome. *Everyone knows the "SSS" will drive you crazy!* She doesn't wish that upon anybody, even Director Ensemble. She must focus; there's important work to be done. She must be able to concentrate on the matter at hand; the students! She's had it before and knows how hard it is to remove once firmly planted. Again and again, it replays. Ms. Treble Clef is desperate! She must break the hold of the "SSS," but she doesn't know how! A loud racket coming from the lobby breaks the hold as the main door swiftly opens. A tall young lady with big brown eyes approaches the front desk. Ms. Treble Clef is relieved it's not Director Ensemble!

Chapter 3
Aeolian and Bassoon

A long-nosed animal enters and approaches the front desk. "Good morning. I'm Aeolian Aardvark, auditioning with Mr. Ensemble."

Ms. Treble Clef looks up. "Yes, Ms. Aeolian. I'm Ms. Treble Clef, secretary to the director. One bit of advice. If you're hoping for a positive audition, I suggest you address him as Director Ensemble; otherwise, your visit will be extremely short."

"Right! Is he ready for me? I'm so excited to be here! I've been up all night thinking about this very moment, and here I am! I visited my grandmother in a nursing facility last fall and heard this incredible sound that touched my heart. I fell in love immediately."

"How delightful. Who'd you fall in love with?" Ms. Treble Clef smiles. "Not who but what! That day, the Appalachian dulcimer swept over my universe like a rug on the floor. My grandmother saw the sparkle in my eyes and gave me the funds to purchase a beautiful teardrop, three-string, walnut dulcimer. I play with a turkey feather, grasping it like a pencil and then gliding it across the strings. Now I make music with a feather and say, '"Gobble! Gobble!"'

Strumming and singing a few bars, Aeolian witnessed the tufts on top of Ms. Treble Clef's hair wilt. "What's wrong? Your hair is falling, Ms. Treble Clef!"

"Oh, that's nothing! My hair has PP! *Not that!* Perfect pitch! Whenever the ends sense music out of tune and not in A440, they fall over. Happens every time! Don't know why, but my hair just does."

Aeolian steps aside and completes tuning with two turns of the silver knobs, using her electric tuner. In triple time, notes of her presentation dance freely in her head, memorized as the composer intended. Suddenly, an authoritative voice reverberates from the office of Director Ensemble.

"Aeolian, enter!"

A bolt of fear shoots down from the tip of shy Aeolian's aardvark nose to her long toenails. She softly strums across the strings to listen to her fine-tuning skill before playing. Entering his office, she starts shivering, seeing the back of his wolfish head. In a flash, he spins around as his thick fur and hazel eyes take hold of her from head to toe, casting a spell.

"Sit! Sit down! Let's get one thing straight. My time is *my time*! When you're in this office, you better be ready as rice in a minute."

"Why, yes, sir. Absolutely. I'm ready to perform my selection, 'Panis Angelicus.'"

A little shaken, Aeolian positions the dulcimer in her lap, turkey feather in hand, and lightly touches the strings. The instrument humbly starts to sing. Music rises to the ceiling with perfection.

Director Ensemble listens without any change in his facial expression. Tears flowing, eyes closed, Aeolian lets her entire soul express the melody. Plucking the last note, she prayerfully bows her head.

Abruptly and without warning, Director Ensemble rises from behind his desk and departs without a word. Aeolian waits for his return and comments. When he fails to come back, she immediately goes to Ms. Treble Clef.

"Is he always that cold? What did I do wrong? Did I pass?"

"Yes, he's always like that! I'll send out a letter with his remarks ASAP. He was listening, and he would have told you in his certain terms what he didn't like."

Relieved, Aeolian picks up her papers and waves goodbye to Ms. Treble Clef. Thrilled to be finished, feeling her oats, she casually bumps into Bassoon Bear from Winfield. "Hey, Bassoon. Are you auditioning today?"

"Yes. Gonna pick 'n' grin my way to a scholarship by showing Director Ensemble what I can do on my banjo. Are you already finished?"

"Yes." It's like playing in front of Mount Rushmore—stone face and no response. He gives you a blank stare, and that's all!"

"Thanks for the warning, Aeolian, but I think I can handle it. I'm a mountain boy, and my mamma raised me to be tough; I can handle just about anything. Can't imagine this director shaking me up so much I can't play. Enough about that. Maybe sometime we can get together and strum a few bars. Here's my number."

Aeolian graciously accepts Bassoon's number, gives a brief smile and a quick wink, and then walks away.

"Bassoon Bear! Calling Bassoon Bear." Ms. Treble Clef's watchful eyes get bigger as they look for the next student. "Last call for Bassoon Bear." Following the sound of a pulsating snore, she finds him in the corner. She's never seen a fellow like this, and her skinny chicken legs are about to snap. "Wake up! It's your turn. Snooze, snore, and lose!" She feels like he might think of her as "finger-smackin' good." Quickly, she tells him to get up and have a seat in Director Ensemble's office.

Shaken enough to stir one eye, Bassoon finds Ms. Treble Clef giving him one of her evil-eye looks.

"Hey, cowboy, where'd you park your horse? Hope you didn't tie him up out front because Director Ensemble will have your hide!"

"What?"

"Well, you look like a rootin', tootin, mighty fine cowboy, dressed in old-fangled denim jeans, leather boots, long-sleeve shirt with special stitchin', and bolo tie, topped off with a fine ten-gallon hat. Figured you had a horse hidin' somewhere. Come with me. Director Ensemble is ready for you. The real question is are *you* ready for *him*?"

Picking up his banjo, Bassoon slowly follows behind Ms. Treble Clef to the director's office. He is wide-eyed and bushy tailed, looking at all the gold records produced by Elmer Ensemble Productions. Having little time to relax, Bassoon decides a friendly greeting will ease tension and hopefully wipe the smirk off the director's face. However, Director Ensemble doesn't even look at him and instead hollers, "Treble Clef! Ms. Treble Clef, I need coffee. Bring it now!"

Right away, she gets up from her desk, answering his call. She knows that if demands of the director aren't met in a certain time frame, life at the academy can and will be miserable. Director Ensemble does not know the word *kindness*. Someone needs to introduce him to a few words like that, but nobody has the nerve. Ms. Treble Clef enters the room with the director's coffee. Missing from her face is the beautiful upward smile that everyone adores but that the demands of her boss frequently draws downward.

"Knock! Knock! Sir, it's me." "Me who?"

"Ms. Treble Clef. Are you expecting someone else? I have your coffee. May I come in?"

Cautiously she enters his office. She's taken aback finding his office chair empty.

Walking in, she discovers the director standing like a statue at the back window. He doesn't flinch as she knocks over his nameplate on the desk. Usually, if she touches the smallest object, his ears stand at attention, and he blows his top. One of the many things he hates is being disturbed. This time, the noise doesn't unsettle a hair on his body.

17

Something has stolen the director's consciousness! He's breathing and standing but unaware.

"Sir, Bassoon is ready for you."

"What? What did you say?" Director Ensemble is looking outside and frowning.

Ms. Treble Clef doesn't realize how invested he is in the outside activity. "Bassoon is here! Ready and waiting. Also, here's the list of students for today. The copy machine gave me back talk this morning, spitting out extra copies. Here they are."

She hands them to Director Ensemble, but he doesn't move; he just continues staring out the window.

The clownfish are at their antics, swishing and swaying to their own type of clownish fun. Dong enjoys dipping under the water to explode upward, waving hello. She repeats the process numerous times. Ding, on the sideline, is applying purple nail polish and planning to redo her large green eyes with sparkling shadow for the day's underwater events. A girl clownfish must always look her circus best, not knowing who's gonna swim by. Crescendo Eel will be in the area today and everybody knows he's the biggest catch in town! Ding and Dong, no further than three bubbles away, are sure to get their eyes full as they swim by.

Bassoon fumbles, putting on his finger picks and quickly retrieving the metal coverings. His banjo is finely tuned in open G. Quickly clearing his throat, he says, "Sir, I'll be performing 'Break Down on Locus Mountain.'" A few starting toe taps, and away he goes, picking just like he's done so many times before. Bassoon and his banjo are like ham and cheese, held together by the love of music. His mother-of-pearl Deluxe Rogue B30 banjo with aluminum rim is a knockout! After a few initial measures, Bassoon's fingers are fully warmed up. Then the "twang rings in all the right places. Director Ensemble's feet tap rhythmically, but his facial expression, well … it's almost like he is afraid his face will fall off if a muscle moves.

Presentation complete, Bassoon anticipates a critique. He is dumbfounded when Director Ensemble shuffles out the door without a word. Perturbed, Bassoon picks up his cased banjo, rolls his eyes at Ms. Treble Clef, and then hustles out the front door.

After a few minutes, figuring Director Ensemble will carry out his usual antics, Ms. Treble Clef goes ahead and fixes coffee before the nonharmonic tones start to roll out of his mouth. Special brew in hand, she enters his office to find an empty chair. "Where can that rascal be? He can only go so far within these four walls and without his coffee."

Checking all the rooms, Ms. Treble Clef finds that the director had reentered the academy through the side door. His eyes are focused, watching two fish, clownfish to be exact. Back again, Ding and Dong are wallowing in the pond, flinging water everywhere. Ding's purple polish glistens across the water as the sun stands high, welcoming the day. Yellow chickadees sing in two-part harmony, and perched crows take notice high above from the wires of telephone poles. The wind whispers a soft melody, encouraging the clownfish to continue their water fun. Unbeknown to Director Ensemble, they are not goofing off but seriously up to no good! Imagine that. Just a couple of real clowns, minus the red noses. Where are their noses?

Bubbles appear again, this time containing letters. Floating around several times, they eventually line up to be read, grabbing his attention: D-I-R-E-C- T-O-R E-N-S-E-M-B-L-E.

The floating illusions appear to contain a message. What does it mean? Four eyes resting on the calm water continue watching over the academy until the director turns out the lights. All is quiet on the water.

Director Ensembles goes to his office, deciding to check out the recent notice from Signature Financial. He's unsure whether he'll open it to read the contents but …

Chapter 4
Coda Crocodile

The night has been seemingly long. Coda Crocodile still tosses and turns as the morning awakens. Her heart is laden with memories of her mom saying, "Coda, you are blessed. Use your God-given talents as He would have you."

Her mother, first chair with the Charleston Symphony, wanted Coda to follow in her footsteps, sensing she had inherited her musical talent. For Christmas, Coda received a cello and immediately began lessons on basic techniques. Coda was a natural. She practiced daily under the watchful eyes and listening ears of her mom, developing tones of an established player. On Sunday mornings, the two played special music during church service. The congregation frequently requests Canon in D composed by Pachelbel, and Coda plays it solo when her mom is unavailable. Coda developed a strong connection to music at a young age. Each piece resonates deeply within her, leaving a special mark on her heart. One morning, tragedy struck when someone broke into their home and stole Coda's cello and bow, followed by the mysterious disappearance of her mom. Coda felt the music ripped from her heart, shattering all family memories. Time passed, and now her heart yearns for music again. "I want to play! I miss Canon in D. This song speaks to me in an incredibly special way. When I close my eyes, I can see the notes on blank pages; I feel them in my fingertips and hear the melody softly playing in my mind. My body unites with the music, giving life. I need my cello. I need it now!"

Constantly the phrase echoes again and again in her mind like a repeat sign in music. Shaking her head in frustration, she cries, "Go away! It's no use. I have no fairy godmother or tooth fairy to wish my troubles away. Besides, they aren't real. Forget about it, Coda! Get real!"

Outside her open window, she hears a dove. "Coo! Coo!" inquisitive Coda looks and finds a white dove.

"Coo! Coo!" The dove lands directly on Coda's large nose. Her eyes cross as she tries to focus on the bird. To her surprise, the dove speaks.

"I've got great news, my friend. A sparrow told me a package is down by the river with your name. Hurry before someone snatches it! Looks mighty fine!"

Coda's eyes light up and widen to the size of watermelons. Arriving at the river, she spots the parcel with her name. Ripping the packing open, she finds a beautiful concert cello and bow, the traditional sheep-gut strings replaced by modern metal. Her body tingles with excitement! No card is present indicating the giver of the gift. She wonders who has blessed her so.

A closer look reveals the instrument is made of spruce, maple, poplar, and willow. The "C," lowest of the four strings, is powerful and rich with sustaining tones. "G" is less dramatic and softer but blends beautifully, being a perfect fifth from "C." "D" is most pleasing, followed by "A," standing out beyond the other three. Tears of joy trickle nonstop down her face. Again she asks, "Who has blessed me? I need to know so I may give them thanks."

More tears flow and she needs more tissues.

Canon's melody flashes back in her mind, giving an encore. The song's lowest "D" resonates inside her, again giving peace that only a musician understands. A peace embraces her body, giving strength beginning with the first note and extending beyond the last note.

As other students arrive at the academy, they notice Coda's exceptional cello.

"How beautiful! Where did you get one so fine?"

"I'd love to tell you, but you'd never understand unless you're a believer."

A harsh voice echoes down the hall, drawing the attention of everyone in the lobby.

"Ms. Treble Clef, where's my next student? Let's keep the pace moving. Hockey begins this afternoon."

Coda's eyes track Ms. Treble Clef as she paces back and forth behind the counter. Coda gathers her cello and bow and follows her to Director Ensemble's office. She enters quietly, and her presence is acknowledged by his big brown eyes looking her over from head to toe. Coda's heart skips several beats, adding a few triple notes, but she carries on. Taking a deep breath, hands positioned correctly, she begins her rendition of Canon in D.

Director Ensemble seems momentarily one with the music as the lower "D" apprehends him with the song's calming effect. Coda tries to get a sense of his impression as he makes notations, but it is too difficult to maintain her concentration. Coda is totally stunned as Director Ensemble abruptly stands up in the middle of section two, slamming the door and abandoning her in his office.

Alone and defeated, she feels like bursting into tears, but who would believe a big crocodile crying, even a girl! No tears from this reptile!

Having exited the director's office, she approaches Ms. Treble Clef asking, "What are you going to do about him? He just walked out on me! So unprofessional. He could have explained why! Didn't his mother teach him manners? Think I'll change my mind about attending here. I bet he's forgotten my uncle John is president of the West Virginia Music Society and is sure to hear about this!"

Coda Crocodile collects her cello and storms out the front door, ranting until she's no longer in view. Ms. Treble Clef doesn't get a chance to say goodbye or give her a schedule. She's never seen a crocodile move so fast.

Director Ensemble returns to his office, awaiting the next student. He hears taps on the back window, and his curiosity convinces him to look. Bubbles! Bubbles floating by his window! Lots of bubbles fill the air. These apparitions have happened once before and now stir and upset the mind of Director Ensemble. He deeply wonders, *Am I losing my mind? Have I lost my mind?*

Rubbing his eyes and reopening them, he sees eight bubbles with letters within, reading "P-A-T-I-E-N-C-E." *Bubbles! Where did they come from, and why are they speaking to me?*

I have no time for this! He blinks again and again, but the bubbles remain. Puzzled, Director Ensemble asks, "Am I losing my mind? I think perhaps, I am!"

A closer look out the window reveals four eyes resting on the water.

Chapter 5
Dawg-Gone Dominant Donkey

Dominant Donkey-Djembe(Drum)

"Still. Still. Still," three words usually nonexistent in the vocabulary at Abington Academy under the direction of Ensemble. He remains in his office watching TV, not knowing four eyes from the pond watch him. The school lobby is eerie and quiet. Ms. Treble Clef is absent from her desk, sneaking snacks from the galley and enjoying a moment of serenity. Dominant Donkey has not arrived for her assessment. Director Ensemble paces back and forth in the studio, promising no second chances for latecomers or no-shows.

"Ms. Treble Clef, bring in my next student. I guarantee you won't like me if I have to wait! Fix my special brew, and bring it along with the student."

Director Ensemble is relentless and calls constantly. Ms. Treble Clef frantically fixes and delivers his coffee, mumbling, "I don't like him. I really don't like him! I'm never gonna like him! Oh well, I do have to eat, even if it's chicken feed."

"Ms. T. C., I'm waiting! I've no time for your dilly-dallying. Where's my coffee?"

Back at the reception desk, Ms. Treble Clef checks her notes. Dominant Donkey is scheduled for this time slot but hasn't arrived with her West African instrument, the djembe, a skin-covered, goblet-shaped drum belonging to the percussion family. Strong fingers and lots of rhythm are required to play this baby! *Sure, leave me out*, thought Ms. Treble Clef. *The only rhythm I've got is in my heart! What could Director Ensemble know about heart? He has none!*

"Where's my next student? I've got important plans this afternoon, Ms. Treble Clef!"

His voice is loud, shrill, and demanding. She can't just go and snatch someone off the street to satisfy him. He storms out of his office, huffing and puffing down the hall. His breath is so strong, pictures fall off the wall. Cup and saucer in hand, Ms. Treble Clef enters the empty office, taking a good look at the executive desk.

"No wonder he can't find his glasses, pens, papers, or anything else. Look at this mess! There's got to be months of mail stacked up! Wait a sec. What's this?"

She notices the edge of an envelope that says, "Superintendent," stirring her curiosity. She wonders, *Should I or shouldn't I? This could be of great importance.* She wants to find Director Ensemble and stick it right up his nose. She really would like to get back at him for all his loud words, but ... she knows that would be inappropriate. She makes an executive decision, pulling the envelope out of the pile, and rips it open! Unfolding the letter, she reads,

Director Ensemble,
It gives us great pleasure to inform you Dominant Donkey has been selected to join the All-City Band. Please congratulate her on this recent accomplishment. Samuel Sitar, Superintendent

Finally, an answer to the Dominant Donkey mystery. *She won't be coming today. Now how to tell Director Ensemble?*

This could be a major problem. Director Ensemble is difficult most days, but today, well, how is she going to explain opening his mail? He's really going to be upset about that! He's probably going to fire me! Searching the academy, Ms. Treble Clef finds the director again glued to the back window, watching the two clownfish. Ding and Dong have returned and are in the lake, flinging water here, there, and, well, you know, everywhere. *If he was closer*, thought Ms. Treble Clef, *he surely would be getting a bath*. Flipping and flopping, having a grand old time, the two clownfish have Director Ensemble chuckling and smiling—almost!

Ding's purple nail polish glistens as the sun stands high in the sky. Yellow chickadees are singing in two-part harmony, while two perched crows enjoy other birds frolicking in the meadow. Music whispers in the mountains. Are you listening?

Chapter 6

Elephant, Eddie étude

Diligently staring at her computer screen, Ms. Treble Clef looks up as elephant Eddie Étude bursts through the front door of Abington Academy. Repeatedly, she hears him say, "I'm late! I can't be late!" His seven-foot, eleven-inch stature is an eyeful for four-foot Ms. Treble Clef. Each of her tiny feathers is so disturbed by his presence they stand on edge, quivering.

Eddie bends down, directly looking into Ms. Treble Clef's eyes. "I'd like to speak to the man in charge."

Shaken but not enough to fly away, she swings her right wing in the direction of Director Ensemble's office.

Nodding in acknowledgment, Eddie Étude stomps (remember he's an elephant) down the hall. Sticking his nose intently in every music door, he's determined to find the correct room. "I know you're here somewhere!" He continues searching until he finds the director. One last studio door remains. Then, in a demanding voice, Eddie clearly states, "There you are! I want to play! I want to play now!"

Entering the room, Eddie slams the door behind him, and now Director Ensemble is stuck with a pachyderm on a mission. Eddie and Director Ensemble end up seated face to face or, should I say, nose-to-nose since both have considerable protrusions between their eyes.

Nary a word is spoken when—*crack!*

"What was that, Director?" Eddie Étude draws his brows down in confusion.

"You should have heard something with those gigantic ears!"

Crack!

"Oh, *that* noise!"

Director Ensemble is 99.9 percent sure the noise originates from Eddie's chair. It couldn't be coming from his chair because he's a member of EG (Elk's Gym), and he's in shape. Eddie's weight is way too much for the little wooden chair, so Director Ensemble decides to hold an abridged session and hurry the interview along.

"Eddie, tell me about your special guitar. Would you mind showing it to me? I understand it has history."

Eddie is ready to show off a little picking and grinning, but—

"Knock! Knock! Pardon me, Director. I'm sorry to interrupt, but you have a call from Marc Lydian. He's demanding to speak with you, now."

"Ms. Treble Clef, you know I'm not to be disturbed. Please inform Mr. Lydo-whatever I'm unavailable."

"Sir, Mr. Lydian indicated this is urgent, and he will not take no for an answer."

"Too bad!"

Frustrated after waiting ten minutes for Director Ensemble to answer, Mr. Lydian disconnects.

Director Ensemble slowly stands, turns his back to Eddie Étude, and exits his office, leaving the student alone. Wasting no time, Eddie picks up his guitar, quickly tunes it, and begins playing several riffs, warming up his fingers in preparation for his audition. Ten minutes into his playing, Director Ensemble returns to listen to the history of Eddie's guitar.

"Sir, this is a 1959 Open G Aficionado once played by Keith Richards of the Rolling Stones. I can't possibly count the number of songs played or strings changed on this magnificent instrument. Love has been spoken on this piece of wood many times. Holding it, I can sense and feel it in my heart. Whew!"

As he hands the guitar to Director Ensemble, his eyes are like those of an eagle. Closely watching, Eddie Étude extends his arms forward, noting whether his nose drips! Heaven forbid nose water on an Open G Aficionado! Eddie Étude makes sure onlookers are not too close and insists that some back up. No heavy breathing is allowed to take place on his music-making machine.

"Wow! This is grand! I'd like to have this baby as part of my classic collection of guitars. What do you say, ole buddy Eddie? How much?"

"Careful, Ensemble! Have you forgotten what you're holding?"

"For heaven's sake, Eddie, I haven't forgotten. I have a remarkable memory. I never forget. Now where did you want me to put this cheap guitar? Maybe you want to sell it to one of the students this year. Congratulations! Welcome to the academy, Eddie Étude. I look forward to working closely with you during your studies. Please excuse me. I've got to run and get back to my students. I'm sure you understand."

"But—"

Abruptly, Director Ensemble leaves his office and scurries down the hall.

Delighted but a bit confused, Eddie Étude collects his Gibson, waves goodbye to Ms. Treble Clef, and goes his merry way out the door. Suddenly, he stops and begins backtracking to the academy. Going directly to the desk of Ms. Treble Clef, he glares at her with his large brown eyes. "Wait just a pretty little minute! I think I've been bamboozled! I never got to audition! I had a great piece of music to share and played not a single note. This Director Ensemble is sly! I think he wants my worthy guitar. Did he pass me to butter me up?"

Ms. Treble Clef just looks at Eddie Étude. She opens her mouth, but no words come out. She closes her eyes in defeat.

Eddie Étude quietly gathers his things, leaving the academy and wondering if admission to the school is worth the value of his guitar.

Chapter 7
Finale Fox

Finale Fox-Finger Cymbals

Finale Fox demands attention walking the halls of Syncopated High. His dark black eyes; rich, furry paws; and downy bib stand out among other student foxes. Classmates move aside, giving him first-dibs seating in all classrooms and cafeteria settings. Lady foxes swoon at the slightest sighting and are eager to push or shove other fox ladies for a glimpse. Everyone assumes his life is fine and dandy. However, his home life is not as grand. Tired of parental nagging, Finale is ready for a complete change. Anxious to live freely on his own, and proud of it, he's forged his dad's signature on applications, obtaining financial aid at Abington Academy.

Sly Finale mastered words on a prize-winning the essay contest themed "*Honesty*." All that is needed to secure his position is passing the face-to-face audition.

Obtaining his bus ticket, Finale leaves for Putnam County and Abington Academy. Arriving early, he can enjoy the beauty of the mountains and breathe the fresh air. His new freedom sweeps over him like a tidal wave. Time goes so quickly, he must hurry to the music department. Checking on his cell phone, he sees he has minutes before he'll be considered late. As he rushes through the door, one flips back, directly smacking him on his pointed nose. Practically in tears, he continues to the reception desk. He pinches his nostrils. Pain is written across his forehead, and tears flow freely.

Finale pulls several tissues from the box on top of the desk to contain the bleeding. Holding his head back, pinching his nose, he grins at Ms. Treble Clef, showing off his large collection of pearly white teeth. Thinking he's still cool among the ladies, he attempts to try one of his high school tactics on the secretary.

Ms. Treble Clef acknowledges his presence: "Finale Fox, I presume. You're late! I'll let Director Ensemble know you've made a smashing entrance. Tissues are over on the round table. I suggest you go and clean up!"

Finale, feeling less than sly, pauses momentarily, thinking of a clever response.

"In the letter, it stated to be on time. Well, I've learned my lesson, so can you throw a little mercy my way?"

Ms. Treble Clef looks up at him with her cornflower-blue eyes and states, "It doesn't matter to me. I have no problem with *your* problem 'cause you've got to worry 'bout the big guy inside *that* room."

Ms. Treble Clef is sure trouble awaits Finale Fox. Director Ensemble is not known for his patience, and tardiness definitely puts him on edge.

A signal on her tablet indicates the director is ready for Finale Fox. Entering, he is greeted by a voice behind a large oak desk. "Sit."

Looking around, he is unsure how to proceed with his audition.

Director Ensemble swiftly turns his chair around, making eye contact with Finale Fox. "Well, well, what have you to impress me with this morning, Fox? Let's proceed. I've no time to waste."

Under the director's deep-set eyes, Finale slowly reaches into a small velvet bag holding not one but two mystery instruments he hope will set Director Ensemble on fire.

Turning his back, he places his thumb and middle finger securely inside each leather strap of the small gold cymbals. He is now ready to show the director and the world his talent. After clearing his throat and taking a deep breath, he presses his thumbs and index fingers together.

"Ting! Ting!"

"What's this? This is what you have? I missed my afternoon of equestrian finals for this? I missed their yearly showcase for this? Get out of my sight before I *ting* you! Gather your tings, pick up your papers from Ms. What's-her-name, and get out of my sight!"

Director Ensemble is not on fire; not even an ember is burning.

Finale scrambles to free the cymbals from his fingers, grabs his papers, and then haphazardly catches his tail in the door. He dares not make a sound but runs out of the room.

Clearing his mind, he decides to walk by the pond. He encounters a clownfish resting by the edge in the sun. Finale rubs his eyes, knowing this is odd and thinking he is dreaming.

Then …

"Hello, Finale, Don't run. My name is Dong. Wanna hear my ringtones? Don't let the unhappiness of Director Ensemble get you down in the dumps. He might not like your cymbals, but don't let him rob you of your joyful spirit. Could the director be jealous that you have happy, and he does not?"

Splash!

Finale blinks. Did he just see a talking fish? Finale has a lot to think about. Has he been staying up too late worrying about this audition, and now he's hallucinating? Perhaps a good night's sleep will clear his mind.

Chapter 8
Glissando Gorilla

Glissando Gorilla-Gong

Not exceptionally smart or known as Miss Congeniality, Glissando always stands out in a crowd. She thrives on attention and manages to draw others toward her as they survey her fashion trends. Waiting like a lion before the kill, Director Ensemble prepares to listen and evaluate his next student, Glissando Gorilla. Ms. Treble Clef quietly opens the director's door and introduces his student. His brown eyes remarkably open as he struggles to maintain composure. Standing before him is a gorilla dressed in a hot-pink tutu, a sight for his sharp elk eyes. The laughter inside him is like a balloon on the brink of exploding! Containing himself takes all his strength.

Glissando opens with one of her big gorilla grins, hoping Director Ensemble will show his lighter side. Unfortunately, he has none. He attempts to uphold his professionalism at all costs.

"Miss, did I hear that your instrument of choice is a golden gum? We don't allow gum in this institution, young lady."

"No, sir. I'm a gong player! Taught by my grandfather, who was one of the greatest in Appalachia. I'm following in his footsteps playing in the mountains."

Director Ensemble looks quickly over at the apparatus but doesn't respond.

Glissando carefully removes the instrument from the traditional covering and lays it lightly on the table.

"Sir, have you seen a gong bowl before?"

Director Ensemble's mouth is overflowing with words of wisdom. "For your information, Ms. Glissando, this is a Tibetan singing bowl, used during religious and spiritual services and meditation by Buddhist monks."

Glissando acknowledges his response, adding a few interesting facts related to her instrument.

"Gently holding the mallet in one hand, you direct it around the outer edges, producing vibrations and rich tones. From a medical standpoint, the singing bowl can improve sleep, lessen pain, improve blood pressure, reduce depression, and enrich lives."

Having explained the amazing qualities, Glissando takes her mallet between two fingers of her right hand and directs them around the outer rim. The tender sound blossoms forth, having zero effect on Director Ensemble.

"I don't need to listen to this … this bowl!" The director stands up and walks out, slamming the door so hard the singing bowl resounds, "Fa-la-la-la-la!"

Frightened, Glissando continues directing the mallet around the bowl, listening to the comforting sound. "Come back! Come back, Director! This is so good! Come take a listen!"

She hears footsteps coming down the hall loud and clear. Director Ensemble is returning, incredibly angry and now standing in the door frame, tapping his foot arrhythmically. "I'm back! What now? My patience is nonexistent!"

"But, but, Director …" Smiling from ear-to-ear, Glissando Gorilla rambles on, "Sir, I want to play in your … what did you call it? Concert or something? This singing bowl has seized my body, mind, and soul. I bet it will seize yours too, if you'll listen."

"Listen to a bowl? Think again!" The director looks at her with his large brown eyes, wets his lips, and opens his mouth, displaying his teeth. "Stop it! Stop it! Stop it! We must move on! I'll consider your request. Take this baking bowl and go!"

"Sir, begging your pardon, *you* told me this is a *singing bowl*."

"I don't care if it's a toilet bowl. I've had enough. Get out of my face, or you'll be wearing this as a hat bowl!"

Glissando picks up her bag and carefully places the singing bowl and mallet inside. She walks to the door without as much as a backward glance at Director Ensemble.

The door shuts, and for a brief period, all is quiet in the mountains.

Chapter 9

Harmony Hippo

Harmony Hippo lives in a neighborhood that loves music. Bursting with energy, she blessed everyone with her rendition of "Happy Days Are Here Again" before the sun had morning coffee. Excitement kept her restless legs consistently dancing in six-eight time long after completion of the song.

This is the morning of her audition. Dad is not happy having to load her concert harp into the back of his Chevy truck. He's worried about scratching his precious baby-blue vehicle. He ought to be concerned about her $100,000 musical instrument.

After an hour of blood, sweat, and a few fears, Harmony and Dad are ready to travel through the mountains of West Virginia to Abington Academy. The plan is to bypass the popular Interstate 64 and take the less traveled scenic route. It's a little longer but will enable them to experience a place like Hawks Nest deep in the mountain.

Finally arriving, Harmony is greeted by Ms. Fermata, who is kind enough to help get the harp through the academy door.

Inside, Harmony is directed to the blue room for a most important performance. The notes she plays today will set the tone for the next phase of her life. Tuned and ready, she warms up by playing arpeggios in major and minor scales, allowing her mind and fingers to lay down the proper mindset.

Director Ensemble rushes into the music room with a deadpan expression on his elk face, demanding Harmony begin plucking those strings. Acknowledging his request, she tilts her instrument back and rests it on her left shoulder. She introduces her selection, "How Great Thou Art," and without hesitation plays. Nervous, she caresses each note, beautifully bringing out sweet tones with volume and expression. Upon completion, Harmony catches a glimpse of the director's face. In her mind, she asks, *Did I just see a small smile? Did my music touch a part of Director Ensemble's heart today?* Pleased with her audition, Harmony jumps up, yelling, "I love music! I delight in giving free concerts because it brings joy and comfort to all."

Observing the expressions on the faces of others, seeing their satisfaction, is something she can't explain. Unless you play, you won't understand that warm and fuzzy feeling you get inside. Music changes things! Music changes you if you open your heart and let it in.

Director Ensemble's face and attitude have changed. His fisted right hand rubs his chin. Briefly, Harmony is afraid his left hand will swing toward her like a pitched baseball from a Yankees player. Instead, Director Ensemble flatly says, "You're done! Collect your papers from the front desk."

Disappointment written all over her face, Harmony gathers her belongings and manipulates the weight of her harp without assistance. Quickly, she leaves the music room, pausing in the hallway. She approaches the front desk.

Ms. Fermata has taken charge. Apparently, Ms. Treble Clef slipped away for a catnap and failed to return on schedule. Director Ensemble will surely have something to say when she returns.

Walking up to the desk, Harmony asks, "What, whatever did I do wrong? What happened?"

Ms. Fermata's eyes met hers. "I'm going to give it to you straight. No sugarcoating and no free space. Don't you know a musician never, ever plays for free? You broke an unspoken rule! A golden rule! Playing for free makes it hard for other music makers to earn a living. Go home. Think about what I just told you."

After exiting the academy, Harmony carefully loads her harp into the Chevy with the assistance of her dad. She is so glad to have passed the audition, but the last comment lies heavily on her heart. Playing for free gives her so much inner joy that it never occurred to her that it infringes on those trying to earn a living. Her heart loves doing for others, and sharing her music is a blessing giving her a loving feeling inside.

Movement catches her eye. Activity on the pond raises her curiosity. Walking closer, she finds two clownfish splashing happily on their backs, swimming, sipping pineapple juice from straws in paper cups. "Slurp!"

Clownfish fun! Then they sing in two-part harmony to the tune of "Jingle Bells":

> Fun, oh what fun! We're having clownfish fun.
> Oh, today! What a day having clownfish fun.

The happy melody is the perfect pick-me-up for Harmony. The frown she is wearing eases upward into a beautiful smile. Her toes start to twinkle, and the urge to dance is hard to contain.

Arriving home, Harmony can't wait to tell her mom all about the interaction between her and Director Ensemble. She talks about the hint of a smile from the cranky ole elk and how he fussed at her playing for free. All in all, she is pleased with herself and the audition.

A phone call later in the week confirms her placement in the academy, but she will not be able to attend the special event in a few days because of the short notice.

Chapter 10
Ionian Iguana

The sky is dappled with the setting sun, and day one's auditions will soon close. Ionian Iguana, a large green reptile, enters the lobby of Abington Academy like a bolt of lightning, grabbing everyone's attention.

Gathering her composure, Ms. Fermata states, "I almost marked you off the list! You're fifteen minutes late! You know that Director Ensemble hates latecomers. I'll check and see if he'll conduct your audition, but I can make no promises."

Momentarily leaving Ionian in the lobby, Ms. Fermata goes searching for the director to no avail. Has he somehow skipped out the back door? How could a large elk with huge antlers get past the front desk? Nobody gets past Ms. F.! Everyone knows cats are notorious for keeping tabs on their surroundings. Their eyes are fantastic spies, and those ears ... well, they hear everything going in all directions! She sure got an eyeful watching that big green thing mosey in. Ms. Fermata instructs Ionian to go directly into the music room to warm up on his Italian flute while waiting for Director Ensemble to arrive.

At her desk, Ms. Fermata pauses to listen as the poetic music played by Ionian flows from the music area to the front desk. Her ears draw forward, listening, as she questions, "Is that J. S. Bach's Partia in A Minor? A beautiful solo partita in four movements containing advanced techniques and more demanding than the Fifth Brandenberg Concerto! Those running sixteenth notes leap from different registers while chromatic descending and ascending arpeggios burst with enormous energy, filling the mind with enjoyment. Wow!" She is lost in the moment when ...

A text message from Director Ensemble comes dashing across her cellphone: "Unable to meet with remaining students!"

Ms. Fermata waits for further instructions but receives none. Zip! Zero! Nothing! Her heart frolics in triple notes, knowing she must disturb Ionian— the big lizard in the music room.

After knocking ever so gently and slowly opening the door, she cautiously enters. Ionian turns his head; his fiery red eyes look up, gazing as if looking through her.

"Yes, you've destroyed my concentration! Now what do you want? This better be good!"

"I'm so sorry to intrude, but there's been a complication. Director Ensemble has been delayed and is unable to return this afternoon. We have your demo, so give me a moment, and I'll prepare your admission papers. Questions, Ionian?" Ms. Fermata doesn't know how Ionian will react, so she keeps her distance.

His eyes lock on Ms. Fermata, and every hair of her body begins to twitch!

"Do you know how long I've been waiting to meet Director Ensemble? My whole life has been centered on *this* day. Now I get a pass! I demand my turn! I want to experience working with the great Ensemble elk! Is this too much to ask?"

Ms. Fermata realizes Ionian is pleading to audition. Not many students beg; most would be ecstatic to be exempt. "I'm sorry, Ionian. Sometimes things are beyond my control; I'm just his secretary relaying a message. We look forward to seeing you at our future event. Be blessed."

Exhausted from the day's events, Ms. Fermata walks over to Ionian and nudges him out the door as she turns out the lights. Reluctantly, Ionian moves, still demanding his turn to play. Ms. Fermata is highly concerned that he might swing his long, powerful tail around and knock her flat off her pretty little cat feet. Everyone knows cats land right-side up, but a swing from his tail could really do harm. She keeps her distance, watching until he's out of sight.

Finally, she can relax her oscillating tail and go take a drink.

Chapter 11

Dynamic Duo

Morning awakens as the sun stretches her golden rays across the mountains. Director Ensemble chose not to return past noon yesterday, following the conversation with Marc Lydian of Signature Financial, which left him befuddled. As he returns this morning, the phone call remains heavy on his mind. The discussion, centering on loan payments or lack thereof, has been addressed via mail, which Director Ensemble has consistently ignored. He knows deep in his heart a problem exists, but he can't face the fact it's time to deal with it. Shuffling under the rug has got to stop!

The reception area has no fresh coffee and cocoa aroma. The front reception desk is missing the friendly receptionists. All is quiet until the antique clock chimes precisely at nine. Day two of auditions at Abington Academy is about to begin.

Director Ensemble walks in asking, "Where's Ms. Fermata? Where's Ms. Treble Clef? Students will be arriving! Who's going to greet and check in the students?"

Ring! Ring!

"Answer the phone! Must I do everything myself?"

Ring! Ring!

"How can I …" Director Ensemble wipes his brow of heavy sweat, wishing he could dispose of all his problems as easily.

Ring! Ring!

"Answer the phone! Oh, that's right. I'm alone!"

The director waits too long, and the phone stops ringing.

Jazz Jaguar is large for his size. His fur is as dark as the night of winter, and his beady black eyes would cause your socks to roll off, but despite his size, he's very personable.

He enters Abington Academy carrying his unusual instrument. A traditional Chinese jiaohu is heard mainly in operas. Director Ensemble's brown eyes stare, taking notice of the odd musical apparatus. Jazz follows the director to the music room for his audition. He hurries to tune as the director is rapping his fingertips on the wall. Director Ensemble's keen eyes give his instrument a worthy glance. The body is round, with two strings tuned a fifth apart and distinctly sounding like a fiddle—for example, string #1 (A) and string #2 (E). Jazz immediately picks up the extended bow and demonstrates a short original piece, not impressing Director Ensemble.

"Are you finished? Go. I'll get back to you. Now leave me be. Ms. Fermata, I need coffee! I need it now! You're going to be jobless if you don't hurry and show your precious cat face. Guess I'll have to get it myself."

Director Ensemble gets up and goes to the kitchen, yelling, "Coffee! I need coffee! Now! Where is Ms. Fermata? Has she used up her nine lives and didn't email?"

Everyone can hear his rambling whether or not they want to listen. His next audition is due any second, and he is not going to start late. From the kitchen window, a commotion on the lawn catches his eye. Unsure, he rushes to take a look. No clownfish this time but a landlubber! A kangaroo is enjoying the fresh air, doing a jig to the beat of 6/8 time! Mystified as to what is going on, he rubs his eyes several times, thinking the vision will disappear. He's completely lost track of time … then—"Students! I almost forgot about my students! Boy, do I need coffee. Fermata, have you abandoned me in my time of need? Come back! Ms. Treble Clef, have you flown the coop?"

The side door slams shut. No one is supposed to have a key besides Director Ensemble and the secretaries. Maybe help has arrived in the nick of time. Which one of them has finally decided to show up?

Dragging her tail far behind comes Ms. Fermata. Her delicate white fur is a disaster. She's dripping wet with bits of dirt and soot all over her. She is a sight for sore eyes and definitely not for Director Ensemble!

"What in the world happened to you?"

Ms. Fermata can't make eye contact. Being high class and proper, she struggles to purr up the nerve to tell him what happened.

"Let's have it, Fermata!" demands Director Ensemble.

Purr-fectly still and sitting tall, Ms. Fermata is ready to tell the tale of her morning. As usual, she walked to work. Taking the shortcut through the wood, Ms. Fermata felt safe so she was taking her time admiring the flowers. She loves looking at all God's creations. Today one of his creatures decided to play naughty. Getting her attention, this human creature of God took the time to pet her ever so gently, so that Fermata thought she'd found a new friend. When she finally felt comfortable, this human picked her up and dunked her deep in a barrel of dirty rainwater. Angry, Ms. Fermata stretched out her claws, trying to scratch the dickens out of this barbaric human. Along came a true friend from the garden, Fred French Horn, the wisest bird in town, who convinced the cruel human to let her go.

Fred made sure Ms. Fermata arrived safely back at Abington Academy. He waited outside, feeling a warm sensation stir in his heart. Something is familiar about Ms. Fermata, but he is unsure why. He dreams of spending time with her but his thoughts are disturbed when he hears a familiar voice, "Now that you're here, Ms. Fermata, get my coffee."

Needing to touch up from all the grit and grime of the situation, Ms. Fermata hurries her tongue along, cleaning her white fur. As usual, Director Ensemble continues to be rude and loud. Everyone can hear his foot tapping to a fast rhythm. "I'm waiting!"

In the kitchen, Ms. Fermata peeks out the back door and sees a hubbub outside on the back lawn. Opening the door, she gets a full view. Unbelievable! A kangaroo, enjoying the fresh air, is dancing the jig to the beat of 6/8 time! Mystified and unsure, she rubs her eyes again and again, thinking the vision will disappear. Again, she hears the deep voice …

"My coffee! Ms. Fermata Cat! Don't keep me waiting!"

"Oh, brother! Not D. E. again! He left out my middle name. I'm in big trouble! Better be sure and pick up a local paper to check out the want ads."

Ms. Fermata quickly fixes and delivers another freshly brewed cup of coffee before Director Ensemble has the mind to release her from his employment. Returning to the front desk, she spots that kangaroo hopping through the front door, heading in her direction.

"Hello, I'm Ms. Fermata. Whom do I have the pleasure of greeting?" "Kapella Kangaroo to see Mr. Ensemble for an audition."

"Yes, I see your name on the schedule. Have a seat, and please refer to him as Director Ensemble. We like to have peace and harmony here on campus."

Ms. Fermata leads Kapella to the music room and attempts to close the door. She is unsuccessful because of her strong tail and finds Director Ensemble pushing on the other side. Winning the tug-of-war, the director forces his way, leaving no time for introductions by Ms. Fermata.

Kapella, the youngest of all those auditioning, stands in fear. Her large tail used for jumping wants to whisk her far beyond the music room, away from the unwelcoming persona non grata, Director Ensemble.

"Young lady, where is your instrument?" he booms. "I've got it right here in my pouch, sir."

"You have *what* in your pocket?" "A kazoo."

Those brown eyes stare at her as his blood rushes upward through his neck veins, flushing his large elk face and turning it beet red!

"You mean to tell me you brought a toy trumpet to audition at my academy?"

"Yes. Is there a problem, sir?"

Chills start to run rampant through Kapella as she stands before the director. The room's silence is overshadowed by her heavy breathing as fear keeps its tight grip.

Director Ensemble is boiling mad. His face is now crimson red; words are stuck to the roof of his sandpaper-dry mouth, and he struggles to speak.

Kapella decides to jet out of the room when—

"Where do you think you're going? Hold those horses, Kapella! We might have something. I hate to admit there's possibly a place for your … what was it? Oh yes, kazoo. I'll have no part, but Ms. Fermata can introduce you to a student who plays some instrument that would sound okay with that thing. Bye."

Kapella quickly exits the music room but returns asking, "Director, where's Ms. Treble Clef? She's not at her desk."

Director Ensemble appears puzzled at her request. Has Ms. Treble Clef been misplaced?

"Guess I'll have to get your papers. Wait here till I retrieve the packet from her file cabinet. There go nine lives!"

Kapella gladly accepts the paperwork and then hops away, leaving the academy. The events of the audition left Kapella unsure. Back at her car, she is now troubled by the noise coming from the telephone wires. Locating the source, she finds two rambunctious crows resting on top of the poles, relentlessly squabbling. Kapella hops over to give them a piece of her mind.

"Is there a problem up there?"

The biggest of the two spreads his wings, looking down at Kapella with his wicked eyes, "You talking to us, sister?"

"As a matter of fact, I am, you lousy noisemakers! I've got a problem. I need to find those two clownfish, or I'm a dead duck."

The two feisty crows look at each other with a big question on their beaks. One responds, "But you're not a duck! Sometimes when you can't find an answer to a question, just sing!"

That crow belts out the first note, and the second crow begins,

Where are the clownfish? I could use a clownfish to
brighten my day.
Where are the clownfish to swim my tears away?
I need a clownfish, a cute little clownfish.
Find me a little clownfish. I need a little bliss!
A little humor can chase the blues away.

Kapella keeps repeating the song, hoping the cute little
fish will make their presence known. She's on a serious
mission, having found two red noses and wanting to return
them. What's a clown without a big red nose?

* * *

The sun beams with happiness. Bubbles reappear as
snoring Ding and Dong sleep soundly in their clam beds,
unaware of activities above. Sun rays travel slowly, waking
up the unsuspecting duo who were up late watching circus
videos.

One high-spirited ray splits in two and shines directly
on Dong's eyes, waking her. Bursting into song, she sings,
"Wake up Ding, sleepyhead, wake up! Get out of that bed!
Wake up!"

Slowly, Ding opens one eye and rolls over, floating
upward, refreshed and ready to face the ocean day of
adventure. Making sure Dong doesn't feel slighted, Ding
swims over to the other clam bed, blows a bubble that
bursts directly over her dearest clownfish buddy, and yells
to the top of her gills, "Get up!"

* * *

Taking a much-needed break, Ms. Treble Clef notices a gentleman walking in from the school parking lot—an odd fellow in bib overalls, dark eyes peeking through spectacles leveled on a crooked orange nose. As he strolls closer, she recognizes him as Fred French Horn, earlier seen at the academy. He introduces himself and then asks about Ms. Fermata Fishing Cat. He lived in the same Westmoreland area as she did until fifth grade. Together, the two of them danced in the street with music provided by his cellphone. Every night, they danced together until their sophomore year when both decided to hang up the dancing shoes and join the school orchestra. Treble had taken clarinet in junior high and by tenth grade was first chair. Fred, however, was known as Mr. Perfect Pitch, as he could easily tell when someone was off just a fraction. However, as a result, Fred had few friends. He later joined a specialty group called Brillante, which traveled with the band. They dated until graduation and then went their separate ways until he rescued her from the mean ole human. Fred doesn't think she recognized him after so many years, but he plans to change that in the near future.

Chapter 12
The Real Thing

It's a beautiful morning in the mountains. The surface water on the pond is calm, and the mountain air is clean and refreshing.

Students waking today are anxious to secure a position and eager to begin their audition. Ms. Fermata arrives and notices Ms. Treble Clef hiding behind a rosebush. "Treble, is that really you? I'm so glad to see you. Boy, have I missed you! Come out, and let's go inside. We've got lots to do."

Ms. Treble Clef doesn't respond right away, not sure if her workmate is sincere since she left her alone earlier to handle Director Ensemble. Slowly she emerges from the underbrush, hiding her face with her left wing. "Please, Treble, let's hurry along. We've got mountains of work to complete before you-know-who arrives."

"He's gonna be so mad at me for deserting his institution! Probably going to clip or set my wings on fire! But I'm here now! I think I see a student. What now?"

"Relax, Treble."

Lullaby Llama walks in the main entrance, carrying her instrument, a lyre. Intrigued, both secretaries nearly fall over each other to get a look at her instrument.

"Lullaby, tell us something about this alluring instrument. We've never seen or experienced anything like it before."

Lullaby is eager to share the history of her instrument. She is out of breath. After pausing a moment, she begins, "The lyre originated in ancient Greece, where the soundboard was made from the shell of a tortoise, arms and crossbar of wood, and the tuning pegs of bronze, wood, ivory, or even bone. Strings could have been from sheep gut, plucked or strummed using fingers or a plectrum made of ivory, metal, or wood."

"Wow! This is fascinating! So much to learn."

With a twinkle in her eye, Ms. Fermata responds, "Play, maestro. Play on."

"Yes, I'll play, but I must inform you I'm rusty, and due to limitations of ancient instruments, you can only play major and minor scales. Should I continue?"

"Go on. We want to hear the timbre of the instrument."

Lullaby stands, picks up her lyre, and places it on her shoulder. She skillfully and methodically plays both in G major and E minor, plucking each note with determination—for example, G major: G-A-B-C-D-E-F#-G-G-F#-E-D-C-B-A-G. After a brief pause, she directly goes into the E minor key: e-f#-g-a-b-c-d-e-e-d-c-b-a-g-f#-e. She doesn't want to confuse them further with the other minor scales associated with E minor going into her rendition of "Little Sunbeam," written by Charles H. Gabriel.

The song speaks to her. Music is powerful, reaching out to our emotions so easily that tears often seep from even the driest personality.

"I need a tissue, please. Ms. Treble Clef, can I please have a tissue?"

Quickly regaining her self-control, Lullaby Llama requests a summary of her playing before meeting the master, Director Ensemble.

Not many at the academy know that Ms. Fermata studied music and was designated a prodigy as a child. Unfortunately, because of difficult circumstances, she was not able to pursue her gift but uses it freely as needed. "Lullaby, measure for measure, the notes sprang individually off the page with perfection. I'm speechless, and I'm *never* without a word."

"Oh, Ms. Treble Clef, I can't wait much longer for the director. My nerves are starting to show up. When is he coming?"

Ms. Fermata joins Ms. Treble Clef in the music room. "We have important news. Congratulations! Relax and celebrate! You passed with flying colors! You came in here like a lamb and are going out having succeeded in your goal."

"Go home, Lullaby. We'll be in touch. Looking forward to hearing you pluck those strings."

Ms. Fermata dismisses herself to get the forms. Ms. Treble Clef wants to give Lullaby a big pat on the back but because of COVID gives her thumbs-up.

Chapter 13

Color Guard

Melody Meerkat arrives at Abington Academy cartwheeling herself right to the front door. Twirling through the door, she ends up eyeballing a tall elk. "You need to watch your step, mister!"

She completes her registration, followed by a greeting from Director Ensemble.

"Hello, sir. I'm Melody Meerkat."

"Why, yes. I believe we just met. What skills do you bring to this institution, if accepted, Ms. Meerkat?"

"Sir, I bring excitement and variety with my African maracas."

"Follow me to the music room, where we can chat and talk about the audition." He sits down and inquires about her maracas. Melody pulls out an exquisite matching pair of hollowed gourds filled with small pebbles. These gourds, believed to have originated from Puerto Rico, were made by the native Indians from the higuera tree. Today, maracas are made of plastic, metal, and traditional wood.

Director Ensemble springs up from his chair. "I've got it! I think I have a master plan for these beans 'n' things. Pick up a packet from Ms. Treble Clef."

Dazed and confused, Melody says, "My audition, sir. What about my—" "Look, kid, I just promoted you to the color guard of the Grand

Performance. What else? Must I spell it out? You passed!"

Stunned, Melody walks out of the academy relieved but freezes in the parking lot, asking herself, "What does this mean? Is this a good thing?" With several questions on her mind, she scurries back into Abington.

Dragging a coonskin case, carrying a replica of a natural trumpet, like those in the Civil War, Nocturne Numbat passes Melody in the hallway. The two start chatting and sharing information about their instruments. Director Ensemble is already waiting in the lobby. Seeing the two together, he asks them to join him in the music room.

Not sure exactly why he asked, the two young ladies follow with hesitation. "Both of you need to become good friends. I have a special mission for you in the color guard. As a duo, you will lead the Grand Performance. Playing your instruments will get everyone in the right frame of mind to stand for Old Glory. This is a big deal not to be taken lightly; the flag must be respected. All students hear about the activity during orientation, and excitement builds. Don't forget to pick up your packets."

Nocturne is trembling with so much excitement she totally forgets which way the front door is located. She runs into Director Ensemble, who gives her a weird look. "Back so soon?"

"Sorry, sir. I forgot my purse. Thanks for everything. I'll make Abington proud."

Director Ensemble is out of the building in a flash. Ready for some quick shut-eye, he heads back to his office. Just as he is about to settle down, he is disturbed by the ringing of his cell phone playing "The Star Spangled Banner." He doesn't want to talk, as he is now drawn to the window by the presence of bubbles! Bombarded by bubbles! Rising and popping so fast he can't read the message contained inside. "Slow down, you bloomin' bubbles! Don't you know my eyes are old. My brain is old, so slow down!"

The bubbles don't care how old he is and keep coming at the same speed, maybe even a little faster.

The message reads, "Director E., it's time you become part of the plan."

Having read the message, he shrugs it off, figuring all this is a result of all final preparations for the upcoming celebrations. He is plum-tuckered tired! Walking over to a mirror, he begins talking to himself, "I'm not part of a plan; I'm the director! I *make* the plans! I *am* the plan!"

Chapter 14
Joy, Joy Joy

Octave Ostrich-Oboe

Following the bubble shower, Director Ensemble is surprised when spurts of water rhythmically start appearing on his office window. Looking out, he finds the two clownfish guilty of observing the director's inappropriate behavior. He is so tired and confused that bubbles are sending him messages. He profusely bangs on his desk, unkind words foaming extensively out of his large elk mouth. Steam escapes from his big ears! He is *mad*! As a matter of fact, he's so mad he's frozen in his footsteps, thinking about being mad when …

Squirt! Squirt! Squirt!

Heavy streams of water reappear on his office window, throwing the director into a rant.

Squirt! Squirt! Squirt!

This time, letters clearly display, "Peace! Peace! Peace!"

Words written in bubbles have so much power that they remain in the air long after the bubbles pop! That's power! Director Ensemble just shakes his head, thinking the day will never come to an end. However, students are waiting for him, and then …

Knock! Knock! Knock!

Octave Ostrich stands outside the front door of the academy, hesitant to enter. Ms. Treble Clef gently goes to the door, opens it, and entices her to come on in. Octave comes in with her precious possession tightly tucked under her fluffy white wing. Cradled securely, her oboe is her ticket into Abington Academy. Ms. Fermata promptly greets her. "Are you on the schedule today, Miss?"

"I am. Can we please hurry this along? I am noticeably warm. A smidgeon delay will cause me great distress." She reaches for a tissue to chase the running sweat but does not solve the problem as more droplets gather around her face.

Ms. Fermata takes time explaining a mix-up in the schedule and that Director Ensemble is running late. She hands Octave a meal ticket to the Perfect Pitch Café for lunch and asks her to return in the afternoon.

Taking her advice, Octave leisurely walks across the street to the eatery and orders a meal. Before she has time to swallow one morsel, Ms. Fermata comes hightailing through the café doors, meowing, "He's back! He's ready! We must not keep Director Ensemble waiting! Octave, move!"

Ms. Fermata gives Octave no other choice and insists she get up without delay.

"What about my free food?"

"Do you want food or an audition? Simple question, so what is your answer?"

A split second later, Octave is running at the speed of a sixty-fourth note back to the academy. Director Ensemble is a quarter rest away from giving up when she blasts through the music room door, entering with sweat ringlets covering her nice white coat and completely out of breath. Director Ensemble remarks, "Well, you decided to come back. Now *play!*"

Barely about to catch her breath, sweat beads the size of quarter notes covering her forehead, Octave is up to the challenge. Praying before picking up her oboe, she hopes her performance of Concerto in C Major by Antonio Vivaldi will blanket any concerns the director might have over her playing skills.

Octave, an accomplished player, has played in numerous settings but never an audition. She finishes and waits quietly for remarks from Director Ensemble. After two hours without a reply, she walks over to his desk and finds him sleeping soundly in his chair. She desperately wants her critique but chooses to tiptoe out of the room without interrupting his triplet snoring pattern.

Three weeks later, a letter arrives from Abington Academy. Octave is both excited and nervous and carefully scans the edges of the envelope. Assessing the number of pages, she thinks extra thin means rejection. She's too impatient to properly open the envelope and tears it to shreds, but the letter is intact:

Dear Ms. Octave Ostrich,

As director of Abington Academy, it gives me great pleasure to inform you, you have been selected to join us as part of our student body. Further instructions to follow.

Sincerely,
Elmer Ensemble Elk, Director

Immediately, she begins singing, "Joy, joy, joy! I've got joy, joy, joy." Sleep does not come that night. Perhaps she has too much happiness. Yes, indeed too much joy! Ringlets now reform, covering her entire body with fluffiness. She looks as though she either has a massive perm or stuck her wing in a light socket.

Chapter 15

All Keyed Up!

Prelude Parrot is ready to face Director Ensemble. He pondered auditioning many times before but insisted his presentation had to be perfect. "The director has never and will never hear anyone like me! He will be impressed when I play! I'll show everyone how piano playing is done! Watch and listen to me!"

He couldn't stop boasting, almost as if rehearsing. Arriving early, he kept reminding himself to remain calm, but today, his mind has a mind of its own. His entire body is at war. Prelude's stomach is wailing the "Hallelujah Chorus." His mouth is dry, and panic has set up housekeeping in his twenty-five bones.

Walking through the academy door, he hears a whisper: "Prelude, you are a great pianist. Do not fear, for God has sent a dove to guide your wings, remembering the pathways of your music. Peace, my child."

Scared motionless, Prelude turns carefully, looking side to side. Being unable to locate the dove leaves him baffled. Time being short, he hustles over to the front desk, where he is greeted by Ms. Fermata.

Escorted to the music room, Prelude is in awe of the magnificent piano before him. Briefly waving his left wing over the keys, he says, "I hope you and I become best buds with multiple opportunities to enjoy your vibrant sound."

The director does not allow "pretickling" of the ivory keys. Prelude has never seen a piano as grand. The instrument is so outstanding that he hesitates to lay his feathers down.

Director Ensemble walks into the music room, makes quick eye contact, and then bellows for more coffee. He checks the piano for music, uttering, "Music, where is the music? Have you forgotten your music?"

"Sir, music? Who uses paper? I never use paper. Besides with all the electronics today, paper is obsolete! I have my own special computer like no other—my photographic memory! A short time ago, I realized not all students are equipped with such a commodity. Shall I begin?"

Director Ensemble nods.

Walking up to the piano, Prelude is suddenly overwhelmed by the size, beauty, and feel of the instrument. Surrendering, he slowly takes a deep breath, releases the air, and cups his fingers over the ivory keys to play.

The music of Pachelbel's Canon in D flourishes with brilliance that would make the composer proud. Bass notes vibrate heavily within the walls while in contrast higher pitches dance lightly around the chandelier suspended from the ceiling.

"Stop! Stop right now!"

The shrill voice of Director Ensemble almost forces Prelude off the piano bench. "What's wrong? Please tell me what I did wrong! I need to know!"

"Hush! Hush right up! I know this piece—note by note. Nothing is wrong. Parrot, drop those feathers, and take a listen to me! We're done. Pick up your packet from the front desk. Scram! I don't want to see those bright feathers until we all meet again, whenever that is. Scoot! Scoot out of here!"

He slams the door with such force the wall shakes, shattering the glass on the director's diplomas. Prelude is disturbed by all the ruckus, but Director Ensemble is totally unconcerned, continuing to his office.

Prelude waves his right wing over the ivory keys as if to say *hello*, hoping he will have multiple times to enjoy the vibrant and beautiful sound.

Ms. Fermata, waiting to walk him down the hall, clears her throat to gain Prelude's attention. She meows, "Have a blessed day. Get plenty of rest. You're gonna need it."

"Coffee! Coffee!" Director Ensemble shouts at the top of his lungs. Back in his office, he's shuffling many piles of mail on top of his desk.

Ms. Treble Clef decides Ms. Fermata needs a break, so she gathers her nerve and fixes the special brew. Entering his office, she notes the pile of mail has grown higher than the last time she ventured in. She bets Director Ensemble has not touched a single piece. Who knows what kind of important information is hiding under the stack? Ms. Fermata knows of the pile but has never mentioned it, fearing the director would probably cut her chicken-feed wages. All that matters to her is a student not losing his or her chance at stardom because of admission papers getting lost or tossed under the rug.

Ms. Treble Clef brings his coffee unnoticed by Director Ensemble, who is busy eyeing the massive pile of mail.

Attempting to organize the stuff, he makes an executive decision: craft paper airplanes and direct them into the trash can. Gotta be more fun than opening mail with less than good news. Planes flying left and right, Director Ensemble is content, relaxed, and quiet. He glances briefly to the right, looking at the remaining quantity of mail, and says, "I'll deal with you later!"

Chapter 16

IQ Quail

Quintet Quail-Quichak

Director Ensemble's stomach is still unsettled concerning yesterday's message in the rising bubbles from the clownfish. The word *mercy* gnaws at him as he eats his breakfast. *What does this mean? Why are they harassing me? I've done nothing to harm them. Maybe they're not talking to me. But who?* The more he tries to forget about the bubbles, the more they pop in his mind.

It is day three of the auditions. Director Ensemble has just arrived and is annoyed at finding the front door locked. "Where's Fermata or Treble Clef?" He begins ranting because they should have been early today with all the festivities planned.

Checking between layers of fur, Director Ensemble realizes he has no key. Walking around to the back, he uses his right hoof to shatter two glass panes on the wooden door. Safely inserting his left hoof, he reaches in, unlocks the door, and turns on a light. "Wait until I grab hold of Fermata's pretty little white neck! I'm dunking her in the barrel of collected rainwater to see how she likes it!"

Ding and Dong Clownfish have gotten out of their clam beds early and just so happen to be observing someone else clowning around.

Director Ensemble is acting bizarre. He's completely unglued without his office companions. He doesn't know anything about the office. He knows his coffee comes from the ladies; he hasn't had any since their absence. How can he possibly conduct auditions without coffee and his secretaries?

The door to the academy slowly opens. A sassy-looking bird hops in and approaches the front desk. "Hello? Anybody working? I've come to audition with Director Ensemble. My name is Quintet Quail. Hello! Anyone here?"

Director Ensemble is listening behind a door. Something about his name strikes an augmented chord. His large nose substantially twitches, detonating a big sneeze! *Achew!* All the audition papers on the desk go flying across the room. He doesn't bother to clean up the mess because he has secretaries (wherever they are) for such minor duties. Instead, he goes seeking an answer:

Quintet Quail, 16
Born in Quebec, Canada
GPA 5.5
Known as the local genius and member
of the High Quality Circle
Early admission Cambridge College
Major: Quantum Mechanics

Reading further, he finds out that at age five, Quintet was considered a musical prodigy. He played Bach and Beethoven sonatas from memory without difficulty. Today, he brings an ancient Iranian instrument—the qichak. With four strings, it is an odd-looking apparatus that is either bowed or plucked. He will perform an original composition titled "Spes Adfulsit," meaning "Gleam of Hope."

Director Ensemble, eager for control, rushes out from behind the door.

"Hello, sir. My name is Quintet Quail. I have an appointment with Director Ensemble."

"Yes, you do. I'm Director Ensemble. Follow me to the music room. I'll give you two minutes to prepare."

Young Quintet follows behind. Exactly two minutes later, Director Ensemble returns to find Quintet with bow in hand, properly seated and ready to showcase his skills.

Open tuning complete, he begins bowing a few notes, followed by a short history, and goes then directly into his chosen selection. Quintet plans to play all ten pages, but after four short measures, he hears, "Enough! Enough! Grab your items. I'll get a packet from the front desk explaining everything." Director Ensemble rushed out of the music room in a flash!

"Coffee! Coffee! I need a cup! I need high test today!" He drags his tail going to the kitchen searching for a hot cup. On the stove, a small pot sits, calling the director's name. Director Ensemble searches the cabinets until he finds one of his favorite cups. He pours and then smells. "Yuck! What's this? I can't drink it! Where's Fermata or Treble Clef? Have they forgotten their duties? Wait till I get hold of your tail feathers or claws!"

* * *

Passing was easy for Quintet, who had performed many times for music juries since age seven. Afterward, he walks over to the lake, admiring the sun as it glistens over the water. A closer encounter reveals two clownfish bobbing up and down, waving. Completely flabbergasted, Quintet trips over a small rock. "Ouch! What? Who?"

"Hello! We are the Doorbells! Would you like to hear our ringtones?" Quintet springs to the edge of the pond, not sure what he'll face.

The small oval body of water is bustling with activity as the clownfish jump up and down. Bubbles float upward again, containing a message: "M-E-R-C-Y! M-E-R-C-Y! M-E-R-C-Y!"

Director Ensemble watches the bubbles for a few minutes and then goes back to the academy, unbelieving and uneasy.

"What's all this mercy stuff? Now where are those two secretaries? After I dunk Fermata and wring Treble Clef's neck, guess I'll have to find new gals for the office."

Hunger takes over, and Director Ensemble goes to the newly opened Doo Wop Café. Walking in, he's overwhelmed with the 1950s decor. Everything is red and silver except for the black-and-white floor that looks like a gigantic game board. Several chrome-plated dining tables caress red or white chairs. Booths are lined up along one wall leading to the kitchen. Retro salt and pepper shakers are included with utensils after orders are submitted. The menu consists of chipped beef on toast, hot dogs and chili, deviled ham, and skirt steak.

Unimpressed Director Ensemble leaves, slamming the door. Safe in the comfort of his home, he heats the skillet, butters wheat bread with oleo, and places thick slices of cheddar cheese on it. Today's mail, delivered through the front slot, remains floor bound as the director refuses to bend. The familiar office technique of kicking, this time under the bed, is his solution. One exceptionally large envelope attracts his attention. Focusing, he hesitates but picks up the correspondence. He feels around each corner, guessing the contents. He already knows but doesn't want to contend with problems.

Heavy rainfall and severe thunderstorms are embracing the mountains. Director Ensemble falls asleep soundly, leaving Abington's problems aside.

Chapter 17
Beginning of the End

The sun waits behind the horizon with her burst of energy to awaken everyone into a new dawn. Excitement fills the air with fresh morning dew hanging gingerly from leaves to weeds.

Director Ensemble is feeling chipper and refreshed after eight hours of sleep. Anticipating a busy day, he eats a healthy breakfast of yogurt, fresh strawberries, and walnuts.

Tired of dressing in style, today, he decides to wear jeans and a T-shirt. His long locks pose a problem as he struggles to pull and comb. Eventually, a ponytail erupts back and dead center. In the far-left corner of the bedroom are ten pairs of various colors and types of shoes. His hoofs must be well taken care of to support his large frame. Before locking the front door, he checks the hall mirror.

Arriving at the academy, Director Ensemble pauses in his vehicle. He rehashes the events of the past two days. So much has taken place, yet there's still much to do. Entering the quiet of the hall, he savors the moment. Talented students will soon enter, and music in the mountains will break forth.

"Where is Ms. Fermata or Ms. Treble Clef? Hello! Anyone here?"

Nothing echoes back; he is alone and decides to try his hand at fixing coffee. Then he sits behind the front desk, anticipating the arrival of students.

The doorknob wiggles, and Ms. Fermata enters, closely followed by Ms. Treble Clef tiptoeing over the threshold.

"Welcome back! Sneaking in, are you? It's a purr-fect time for you to return and get to work! We have students arriving! No dawdling!"

Grabbing the list, Ms. Treble Clef's tail happily sways back and forth as she anticipates the students. "I'm so excited. I can't wait to see them. Everyone has worked so hard to make this school a success."

"Speaking of work, are both of you forgetting something, Ms. Treble Clef? Coffee! Which one of you is going to get my coffee?"

The two secretaries look at each other and shrug their shoulders. Ms. Fermata volunteers, and Ms. Treble Clef remains at the desk.

"Where's Rhythmic Raccoon? The first student hasn't arrived, and already I'm late! You know how I feel about that! Get my coffee, and bring it stat! I'll be in the music room, waiting!"

Ms. Treble Clef doesn't have time to respond before a short, rough, ragged raccoon ventures through the front door. "I've been roaming around, and by golly, I got lost! Beggin' your pardon, Miss, but am I too late? Cause I know I'm supposed to be on time."

Looking over the counter to speak eye to eye, she says, "You were just about to be deleted. Where's your instrument?"

"Oh, I have 'em. I never, ever travel without my sticks. I can't eat or sleep unless I have 'em near me. Then I can practice my craft anywhere I go."

Walking together down the hall, they hear Director Ensemble pacing and grumbling, "Wait until I get hold of Rhythmic Raccoon! He will not have a place in this establishment no matter how good he is. He knows the rules, and being late is a major infraction!"

"Knock! Knock! Director Ensemble, it's Ms. Treble Clef. Rhythmic Raccoon has arrived. Should I send him in?"

"Send that varmint on in, and be ready to rock 'n' roll with his things." "Rain sticks, sir." Rhythmic Raccoon enters, tilting his sticks up, down, and

around, simulating the sound of falling liquid sunshine. Without delay, he begins belting out a song, "Rain, rain, don't let the rain come down …"

"Really! Do you call that music? Whatever; just get that noise out of this room ASAP. Collect your information from Ms. Treble Clef. Vamoose!" Rhythmic leaves the music room, heading directly to the front desk.

Newly at the desk, Ms. Fermata is trying to compose herself, holding in the biggest laugh possible. "Boy, you wrinkled the director's antlers like nobody I've ever seen. Congratulations!" Ms. Treble Clef gives a thumbs-up to the student before Ms. Fermata leads Rhythmic toward the door. Still holding his rain sticks, he shakes and rattles, making music while leaving the academy.

The secretaries continue talking quietly long after Rhythmic Raccoon has faded from their sight. Neither of them had experienced a student get the best of Director Ensemble in a whisper of time.

Chapter 18
Upside Down

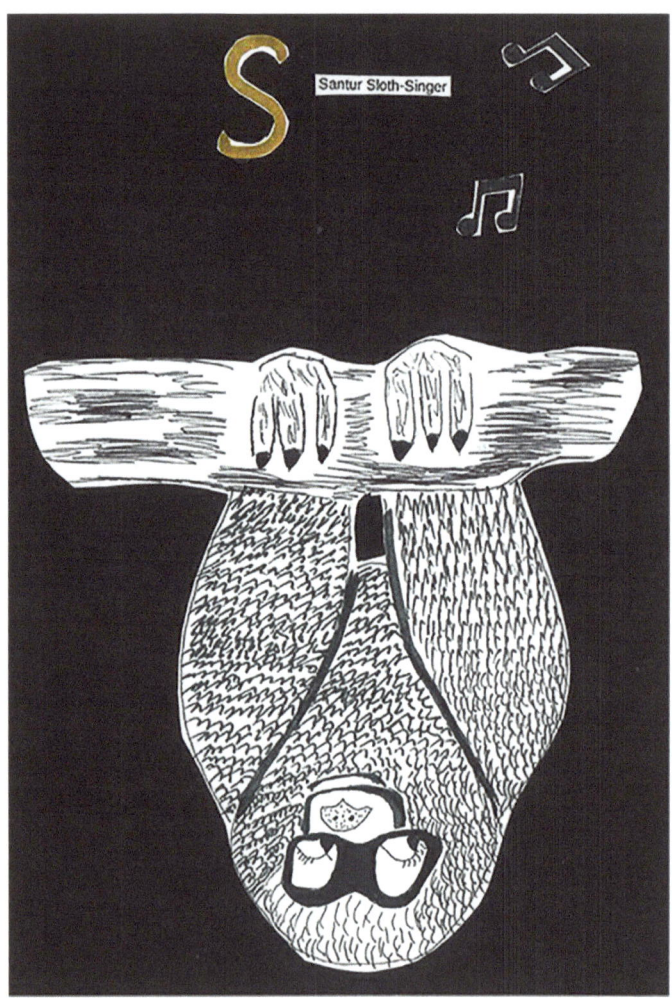

The night has dragged on. The moon in all its fullness has hampered Santur's normal deep sleep. She tosses frequently, unable to relax even with the old-time favorite of counting sheep,

Santur Sloth struggles to rise the morning of her audition. Most mornings, she completes a series of yoga tree and freestyle poses for stress relief but not today.

Upon her arrival at the academy, Ms. Treble Clef directs Santur to the auditorium to begin warm-up techniques on her vocal cords. As a seasoned community theater performer, she's ready! Wetting her lips, standing tall, she inhales a low, deep breath and then … nothing! She waves at Director Ensemble, who gives her a strange look. Taking three steps back, Santur waves to two stagehands in the corner with a puzzling, whispered request. Shaking their heads, they disappear, walking toward the large utility closet in the back of the music room. Within minutes, they return, dragging a metal coatrack on wheels.

Impatient as always, Director Ensemble instructs Santur to hurry along because of an important TV program coming on SPIN.

"I cannot be rushed! I have only one speed: slow!" says Santur. After adjusting the microphone and wetting her lips, she says, "Lights out, please," a small but important cue before something beautiful.

"Ave Maria" begins encompassing the room. Director Ensemble searches for the origin of the sound. Slowly, a gentle light reveals the source hanging upside down. The director and others stand listening to the range, quality, and quantity. His eyes wide open, he attempts to focus on the image hanging from a coatrack. A closer look identifies the shadow as Santur Sloth.

In his mind, Director Ensemble questions what his eyes see. How could a slow, small creature upside down produce sound so pure?

What follows no one would believe if they hadn't witnessed it themselves. Director Ensemble is standing, clapping, and hollering, "Bravo!" for Santur. Never, ever before has this happened at Abington Academy. Never has Director Ensemble stood up and clapped. What a day! The mountains of West Virginia rejoice in song, this time louder than a whisper.

Righting herself, Santur is embraced by both Ms. Treble Clef and Ms. Fermata.

"Will we hear this again, upside down?"

Forgetting their requests, she immediately turns to Director Ensemble, questioning, "My audition, did I pass, sir?"

Director Ensemble smiles and replies, "I'll never forgive you if you don't, and yes, you passed!"

Both Ms. Treble Clef and Ms. Fermata are in shock! Kind words are flowing out of the director's mouth!

"I hope I can do this again, as I just surprised myself. My voice is so fragile. I must be careful not to strain. I usually perform only once a day because it takes strength to sing. God, who is all loving, gives me strength each day. God's grace will bless me once again to rejoice in song." Slowly lowering herself and releasing her grip on the coatrack, Santur gladly accepts passing the audition. Still in awe, the two secretaries stop Santur and congratulate her before she leaves the building.

Chapter 19

Triad Tiger

Triad Tiger-Tuba

Triad Tiger has grown up along the Kanawha River with his parents and siblings. The youngest of five, he is often home alone while everyone else attends practice or games. Being young and frequently by oneself can offer many opportunities to get in trouble. However, Triad manages to whisk away the daylight hours participating in his favorite activity.

Triad loves being outside with all things creepy crawly and dreams of being an entomologist. After school, he goes out searching for happy bugs, leaving rocks and pebbles upright for titanic creatures to scare little sisters or other neighborhood children. Full of energy, he loves fresh air, solitary play, and climbing the old oak tree beside the patio, where most of his daylight hours are enjoyed.

Dad built a swing outside his bedroom window, not knowing he would sneak out for a swing to enjoy the stars or capture night crawlers. Daytime hours are spent watching local boats transport coal down the Kanawha River. Triad attempts to encourage the boat captains to blow their horns, jumping up and down as they pass.

Red House Shoal is found off Route 62 between two mountains. Local folks tell visitors not to blink, or they'll miss all the action. During spring, melting snow trickles down the mountainside, making unique songs. Are you listening?

In junior high, Triad joined the band; hence his bugs take a back seat, and a tuba moves in as best friend. Inseparable from his tuba, Triad practices day and evening. Since his introduction to music, his folks must remind him of bedtime, as he gets lost in rhythms and intervals, wanting to spend numerous hours in study. He selects the sousaphone, the tuba designed by John Philip Sousa, for the warmer tone and bell shape for better projection.

During sophomore year, he receives an award for Most Improved Brass Player and decides to apply to Abington Academy.

On the day of auditions, Triad looks like a true "fraidy" cat, knees knocking, teeth chattering, and his heart thumping in various rhythms, surely out of sync.

Arriving at the academy, Triad is welcomed by Ms. Treble Clef, who directs him to the music room. Director Ensemble enters with a strange look on his face.

"Triad, do you hear anything? I hear cracking."

"No, sir." Triad crosses his legs, keeping his knees still.

"Uncross those knees! How do you expect me to hear your tuba?"

Rats! Triad thinks. He knows trouble is brewing. His lips are quivering, but at least they are silent! Uncrossed, his knees begin jumping like beans, possibly preventing him from playing. Lips in place, proper breathing and nothing! He doesn't know what to do, but he remembers to keep on trying because that's the sign of a true musician.

"Get your act together. I shall return in a few minutes," says Director Ensemble, slamming the door to the music room.

Triad's eyes begin welling up with tears the size of watermelons. Disappointment and frustration paralyze him. Will he get another chance? Today is the last day, so when?

Director Ensemble reenters the music room fifteen minutes later, instructing Triad to try again in the afternoon or forget about placement.

Triad Tiger nods in response, places his tuba in the case, and then solemnly walks down the hall. He has never received a rejection; this slaps him hard. He wants the audition to go smoothly so he can continue his dream of attending the academy. God must have another plan, so accepting defeat, Triad continues out the front door without looking back.

* * *

The morning session has been long and wearisome. Director Ensemble can barely keep his eyes open; he tries toothpicks, but they snap, failing to do their job. He thinks about going down to the café for a break but decides a walk with relaxing and fresh mountain air will probably provide more of a boost rather than a heavy meal, which could weigh him down.

Fifteen minutes into the stroll, Director Ensemble finds a quaint little nook hidden down a small alley called the SaucerMan. Inside, this little cubbyhole is remarkable. The wooden floor is damaged with stains and black marks. The walls are aged and desperately in need of fresh paint. Cobwebs freely hang from light fixtures patterned heavily with dust. One antiquated fountain grabs his attention, reminiscent of the soda stand era. On display in another area, the entire wall is covered with saucers. Wiping off the thick powder reveals eighty gorgeous saucers with gold rims made by English Rose.

For a moment, Director Ensemble is transported into another era until he is interrupted by his ringing cell.

"Mr. Ensemble, Marc Lydian, Signature Financial. Sir, I'm afraid you've ignored all my correspondence, and now I've no choice. Bankruptcy papers are inevitable. I'm sorry, but there's nothing else I can do. Expect delivery this afternoon."

Director Ensemble hangs up, not wanting to hear any bad news. He glances at his watch. "Oh, I'm late! I need to make major elk tracks back to the academy. Students are waiting."

Back at Abington, Ms. Fermata is busy with office work when she realizes Director Ensemble has not returned. "Ms. Treble Clef, have you seen the director?"

"No, not for at least two hours. He left not telling anyone where he was going. I wonder where he is. Students will be back in a few to finish auditioning."

"Where could he have gone? He knows students will be returning. Ms. Treble Clef, do you know anything about music just in case the director fails to return?" inquires Ms. Fermata.

"No, I'm completely clueless as well as tone deaf, so don't ask me! But, Ms. Fermata, weren't you a child prodigy? You must know something about music!"

"Yes, yes, but that was very, very long ago, and my musical memory has faded somewhat. Guess we better hope he shows up on time. Let's wait and see what happens."

Director Ensemble decides to take a detour before heading back to the academy. The call from Marc Lydian has had an adverse effect, and he begins to rethink his method of hiding his problems under the rug. However, at the moment, students are waiting, and he must return to the academy for the business at hand.

Chapter 20
Amazing Music

 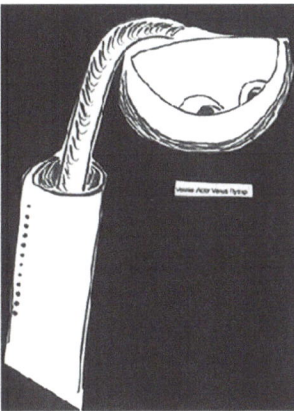

Upbeat Uakari has been harassed since birth because of her appearance. A gentle giant with long, straggly hair; a toasted face; and a shiny bald spot in the center of her head, she is still part of God's plan. Today is special because Upbeat plans to step out of her comfort zone for an adventure beyond all dreams.

When she wakes up this morning, the sky is stormy, raining cats and dogs. Cute cats but some of the dogs give Upbeat a run from the nearest hydrant. She has plenty of time on her massive hands before audition, so she decides to wander about her newly purchased older home. Within minutes, she finds an extra-large closet located in the smallest bedroom by the pond. Curiosity takes hold, persuading her to check out the space. One swift kick with her right foot and whoosh! Massive amounts of dirt start flying. After picking up and turning on a flashlight, she enters the dark space. Laced cobwebs line the walls from top to bottom. *Crunch! Crunch! Crunch!* with every step. Even the black area has musical inflection! "What am I stepping on? Hope it's not water bugs 'cause I hate water bugs! Walking on 'em reminds me of eatin' tater chips. I love tater chips! Mmm! One's not enough!"

Upbeat keeps crunching in the closet until something triggers her arm hair to rise but not shine. "What, what's that? Is someone over there?" Trembling, Upbeat shines the light in the area of movement.

A strange voice calls, "You bet something's over here—me!"

Alarmed, Upbeat again shines her light! Two big green eyes stare back, causing the flashlight to cease shinning! No more crunch time, as Upbeat is now in fear. Words refuse to form in her large mouth. Her long, stringy hair stands straight up, shivering in fright. A raspy voice shillyshallies from behind the door. Clearly and without delay, it says, "Staring's impolite! Was your mamma short on manners? Water bug got your tongue? I'm the new kid in the closet, Vennie Venus Flytrap. Who are you? Say something! Loosen up, or you'll never pass that audition. Listen to me! I go back centuries in the music business. You want to pass that audition, don't you? We fly-traps regenerate, you know, over n' over—forever."

"Okay, smartie, tell me something about yourself. My inquisitive mind wants to know."

"How much time do you have? I've got a story to tell, so you might just get comfy. I was lead singer for the Grass Tyme Fever Band before we got mowed over by Big Green

John, a nice guy who got carried away doing the lawn. It was the weekend of July 4, and he was listening to music with those ear things and got carried away, mowing right over us during the refrain of "The Star Spangled Banner." Now we just sit around among the weeds, listening to the crickets chirp. While I'm on the subject, would you like a few pointers or notes on passing your audition? Won't cost anything."

"Okay, all right, but hurry up!" mumbled Upbeat.

"In the music business, you have to have an introduction. Begin with a simple smile; takes less muscles than a frown. Raise those red lines below your nose! Smile! Smile! Smile!"

Upbeat's brown eyes opened wider than the entrance to Lincoln Tunnel. Her lips opened, displaying colossal teeth, needing a dental hygienist! Vennie's eyes locked on Upbeat.

"Who wants to look at anything unhappy and, in this case, needing a toothbrush? Brush those teeth, use mouthwash, and then smile!"

Upbeat shuffles about, looking for her toothbrush. Thirty minutes later, she locates her mouth cleaner concealed under large amounts of her shedding hair. Upbeat hustles, tediously removing each strand from the brush until it is free, clear, and ready for cleaning.

Teeth brushed, Upbeat leaves for Abington Academy with renewed energy and a sparkling clean mouth. She walks to the mirror, admiring her smile. Ms. Fermata uses her tail to shield the brightness of Upbeat's teeth. "Director Ensemble is waiting. I suggest you get going."

An odd sound dances from underneath the door … *ta-ta-ta-ta-ta*! Ms. Fermata cautions Upbeat, stressing that rhythmic patterns are a sure sign Director Ensemble is agitated. Swiftly, she opens the music room just long enough to scoot Upbeat forward and then slams the door. Upbeat is facing Director Ensemble. He is not happy, although his hoof is silent.

"It's a beautiful day! Don't you love to smell the fresh air, hear birds sing, and feel wet grass on your hooves? Waking up in God's wonderful earth among all His creatures is a blessing. Don't you agree, sir?"

Looking over his glasses, Director Ensemble has had plenty of her wordiness. "Forget this nonsense, and for Pete's sake, silence! I'm in charge! You are to listen, learn, and follow directions!

Giving the student one of his looks, he says, "For heaven's sake, quit smiling and not another word. I do the talking! You are here to listen and learn, follow directions, and do whatever I say. Oh, now you can tell me about your instrument, but make it quick. I have a sports date."

She must choose her words delicately, refraining from any sign of happiness. Taking a monotone voice, Upbeat begins, "Sir, these are uilleann pipes, the national bagpipes of Ireland, bought by my parents, who thought they'd shut me up! They took the time to teach this marvelous instrument to me. Maintaining a steady flow of air is key. I figured this would be easy since I can rant surprisingly well. Shall I play for you? I'd love to play 'Amazing Grace.'"

"I understand now why your parents wanted to close your mouth! You have an abundance of hot air! Why aren't you floating?"

Before dressing herself within the confines of the bagpipes, Upbeat decides to share the history of "Amazing Grace."

"The composer, John Newton, was captain of a slave ship. During one voyage, the ship encountered a dangerous storm on the high seas. On the brink of disaster, John Newton decided to pray, asking God for safety. God heard his prayer, as he hears all, and saved the ship from sinking. On solid ground, John was so thankful he repented his sins and gave up his duties as a slave trader, later becoming a minister." Bowing her head, she pauses a few moments and then begins playing.

The notes fill every space of the music room with richness and beauty. Director Ensemble fights tears as he listens, something he's never, ever experienced before. A small, exceedingly small, smile appears on his face, and a tear sits in the corner of his right eye. Does this song have a special message for Director Ensemble?

The pipes are now silent. Upbeat looks up. "Well, sir, what do you think?"

Director Ensemble looks directly at the student before him. "Fine, that was mighty fine. I'll search for a place in the program for your instrument. Be prepared to play exactly as you just performed. Ms. Treble Clef will give you the needed information."

Leaving the music room, Upbeat notices Director Ensemble wiping a few tears from his face. Has he been touched by the music or something far greater?

Viola Vervet-Violin

The afternoon turns stormy as dark clouds gather and the winds begin to blow. Secretaries Ms. Fermata and Ms. Treble Clef are weary and ready for the day to end, completing the auditions. Presently in the lobby, Viola Vervet and Waltzing Wallaby anxiously wait their turn to meet with Director Ensemble. Chatting like old friends, they only met on the bus coming from Huntington. Both young ladies attend local high schools but in different areas of the large city. Viola, a sophomore, a member of Vinson, plays piccolo in the marching band. Waltzing, also a sophomore, attends East Huntington and had just been appointed to the varsity cheering squad when she was notified about Abington. Both are about to venture into the new world of Ensemble, and having a friend to lean on would be beneficial, despite their high schools' history of rivalry.

"Good afternoon, ladies. May we have your names?" Ms. Treble Clef asks, sitting at the front desk alongside Ms. Fermata.

"Yes, I'm Viola Vervet, and I'm Waltzing Wallaby. We are both here for auditions with Director Ensemble."

"Yes, we have your names and will be right with you. Relax. Director Ensemble will be here shortly."

Director Ensemble walks quietly through the door, views the students, and without much ado motions to the secretaries as he walks to the music room.

Ms. Fermata follows to answer his request and is shocked when he politely asks for coffee. Stunned, she leaves to collect his perfect cup of morning juice.

Ms. Treble Clef waits for him to summon one of the students before sending in either Waltzing or Viola. Both secretaries are puzzled by how quietly the afternoon has begun. However, there's so much to do and so little time.

When Viola is called, she is ready for the task at hand. Taking her instrument out of the case, she walks down the hall and gives herself a little pep talk. "I can do this! I can do this! I really can do this!" Her instrument, the violin, is made of ebony, a hard black wood. All wood used for this instrument, which includes maple and spruce, must be dense and strong. The violin has four strings: A, the highest; C, the lowest. The instrument sounds lower than a viola but higher than a cello. It is also known as the Cinderella of the orchestra because it is frequently overlooked in musical compositions. Preparing her proper mindset, she rosins the bow, plays several sets of scales, and decides to include the harmonic minor for a complete change, making sure to raise the seventh tone one half step. Finally, adding a few improvisations, she limbers up her fingers for the audition.

Twenty minutes later, Ms. Fermata scoops up Viola and takes her to the director's office. "I'm sorry to disrupt and bring you in here, but they decided at the last minute to clean the music room. I hope this won't cause you any problem."

Being alone in the director's office increases Viola's nervousness tenfold. She takes a few minutes to notice the large picture window on the back wall. Opening the blinds, she says, "Wow! The Appalachian Mountains!" Immediately, she is projected into a twilight zone of relaxation. Fear and anxiety vanish as easily as flipping on a light switch. Turning around, she notices a large roll-top desk of solid oak with a matching file cabinet that includes a brass engraved plate: "*Elmer Ensemble, Director.*"

Totally engrossed in the room, forgetting the director might walk in and witness her wandering around in his personal space, she continues. On another wall are graduation pictures and a diploma from the University of North Carolina with a master's in music education, magna cum laude.

Suddenly, a strange sensation falls over Viola, giving her the creeps. *I've never had vibes like something crawling all over me, and I can't explain this sensation*, thinks Viola. *Is someone watching me? Are there cameras in here?*

Tap! Tap! Tap! There's tapping on the window from outside. Then a voice says, "Can you please help me? Please raise the window, and let me in. Pretty please with Splenda on top! I'm watching my figure. Hello, I'm Vennie Victor. I'm so hungry I could eat you! Relax, I won't do that, 'cause I'm friendly."

Viola can't scream because of her mouth being as dry as the Gobi Desert. Instead, she skedaddles out of the director's office quicker than a bolt of lightning. Looking at the other students in the lobby, she asks, "Did you see that … that thing? It wanted to eat me!"

The students shake their heads negatively and snicker under their breaths at Viola, giving her the weirdest look. She returns to the director's office and closing her eyes says, "I didn't see anything! I didn't see anything!" She slowly opens her right eye and then the left. Gone! It's gone!

Now that it is gone, she has little time to concentrate on her audition before Director Ensemble arrives. Prepared to play, she draws a blank! "Oh no. Now what? I'm really nervous, and he'll be in here any moment. Dear Lord, I could really use some help!"

Silence is deafening when squirts of water start appearing on the back window in three-quarter time.

Squirt! Squirt! Squirt! Squirt! Squirt! Squirt! Squirt! Squirt! Squirt!

"What's this? What could this mean? This has a kind of waltz feeling. That's it! I'm playing 'Waltz of the Flowers' by Peter Tchaikovsky. Thanks, whoever you are."

Grasping her instrument and bow, she sits down and begins her mental preparation. Closing her eyes, she waits for the notes to appear in her mind, but a blank piece of sheet music appears. Viola quickly opens her eyes and raises her arms above her head. "Dear God, I need you. Refresh my memory so that I may play giving all the glory to You." Quietly, she waits. Notes begin filling her mind and then travel down to her fingertips. She's ready to begin as Director Ensemble enters the music room.

Now relaxed, the music flows from her violin with grace and beauty. Director Ensemble listens intently without uttering a word but does not leave the room. He remains silent as Viola packs her instrument and quietly exits the room. Ms. Fermata waves goodbye as she leaves but is mystified why Director Ensemble has not returned to the lobby.

Chapter 22

Waltzing Wallaby

Waltzing Wallaby-Washboard

Waiting her turn, Waltzing Wallaby sits in the far corner talking to herself. "I hope Director Ensemble is ready for me! I'm special; all the cheering gals are special—just ask!"

Ms. Treble Clef hops over to chirp or sing since her beak doesn't extend into what one considers a welcoming smile.

"Hello, nice to meet you. I'll be introducing you to Director Ensemble down in his office. Please follow me."

Waltzing anxiously hops behind Ms. Treble Clef. Entering the music room, Ms. Treble Clef finds Director Ensemble sitting quietly in the dark. She turns on the light, and momentarily he appears to be in a trance. He is unaware of her presence, and his eyes are focused straight ahead. Ms. Treble Clef cautiously approaches him, saying, "Sir, I have your next student."

He blinks, shakes his head as though back in reality, and replies, "Certainly. Have a seat, and make yourself comfortable."

Waltzing makes herself comfy, sharing one of her happy faces. "Nice to meet you, sir. I've waited a long time to be here at Abington. It's a beautiful afternoon, wouldn't you say, sir?"

Director Ensemble's expression says it all. He is not impressed with her attitude and immediately wants to set her straight. "First and foremost, miss, don't you forget who's in charge! That would be me! Second, if I say move, you better advance fast and correct. Third, my rules are to be followed. Four, questions, keep them to yourself. Waltzing, are you prepared to perform on a moment's notice?"

"Absolutely, sir. Shall I begin?"

"Wait, wait just a sec! We speak only one language at Abington. That would be the language of Ensemble. Learn, and learn fast! Excuse me for a brief coffee break."

Director Ensemble stands, pushes his chair aside, and quietly closes the door to his office. Waltzing is stunned! Abandoned just as she was about to perform. "Well, I've never been treated so rudely! I know to whom I can report his obnoxious behavior, and by golly, I'll do so."

Waltzing's self-esteem shrinks to the size of a grain of salt. She could trip over her lower lip if not careful. She is crushed to nothingness.

Alone she thinks she hears noises. Maybe her mind is playing tricks. Maybe the entire day has been too stressful. She goes outside for fresh air and a small snack to raise her blood sugar. Perhaps that's all she needs to perk up. Having grabbed her instrument, a washboard, Waltzing begins strumming a few bars, using the hard tips of her paws. The metal sound, not having a true pitch, is rough and loud. Critters resting in trees outside take flight, seeking quieter areas.

Returning, she finds the academy door locked! Mad as a hornet, she bounces up and down, breaking the support strap of her washboard around her neck and causing it to tumble down a small embankment. Stunned at the loss of her instrument, she initiates a secret rule of songwriters. When in a sticky situation, do three things: 1) make up; 2) carry on; 3) sing along. Easy enough. Waltzing knew immediately what to do to calm her restless spirit. She started singing like a songbird. As an amateur songwriter, she composed,

Where oh where did my washboard waddle to?
Where, oh where, wonder where?
I need my washboard to clean my clothes,
Washboard, please wobble waddle back to me.

A low, haunting voice wanders into her mind. "Director Ensemble's not gonna like your washboard! It's not even a real instrument! It's not conventional! What were you thinking? Whatever gave you the idea he'd let you play in his very fine establishment? He will insist you take it where it belongs—wherever that is! He's gonna throw you out! He's gonna call you names!"

Looking around, she searches for someone or a key to let her in. She knows that this is her only chance to audition, for there are no second chances at Abington. Unsuccessful, Waltzing wonders what else to do. A sweet voice inside her head says, "Waltzing, don't give up! Don't be afraid. Musicians have unspoken rules. God is with you from the first note until the last. Remain calm, and keep those fingers moving. If you lose your place, God will send you notes to fill in the lost ones. Maintain composure no matter what! Never make a face! Remember, God is in control!"

Waltzing scrambles to find her instrument while trying not to be discouraged. As the sun starts to settle behind the mountains, she notices a reflective light coming from a tall oak tree. Searching, she finds her washboard wet and dented but thankfully in one piece. Breathing a sigh of relief, she knows she can fix her instrument. *I can dry it and then polish out the rough spots with good ole spit, but I've got to hurry. Director Ensemble will not wait. It's time to make music!*

* * *

Back at Abington, Ms. Fermata greets Waltzing. "You look different— strong. How did you make such a change? We better hurry down the hall. Director Ensemble is waiting."

Entering the director's office, Waltzing meets his gaze. "Director, I challenge you to pick up your instrument and let's jam!" The look on his face is pure disbelief; a student has never wanted to overtake Director Ensemble and engage him in playing music! Wow!

Secretaries Ms. Fermata and Ms. Treble Clef stand in the doorway.

"I don't believe my ears! In all my years at this establishment, I've never seen or heard the director pick up his instrument and play alone or with one of his students!"

"Oh, did I see a smile? I've never seen that either! What a day at Abington!"

Director Ensemble and Waltzing begin singing duet style and are then joined by the two secretaries. Music in the mountains fills the air. Everyone is relaxed and happy. At the end of the session, Ms. Fermata hands Waltzing her packet, reminding her of the program to be scheduled at a later date.

"Ms. Treble Clef, can I please have some coffee? All this singing has my throat parched."

Ms. Treble Clef can't reply to the director's request because she is in a state of shock at hearing the word *please*. However, Ms. Fermata goes to the kitchen and fixes a special cup of coffee in his special cup.

Coffee in hand, Ms. Fermata finds the director looking out the back window in a daze. "Sir, sir, I have your coffee. Where would you like me to leave it?"

Ms. Fermata waits a few seconds for his reply, but he is completely spellbound by bubbles floating and rising from the pond. Thousands of illuminating bubbles stream upward, forming a message: "Blessed are the meek."

Director Ensemble walks solemnly back to his office, welcoming the few   remaining students.

* * *

Secretaries Fermata and Treble Clef gather in the kitchen to discuss the new behavior of Director Ensemble. Neither knows what has changed his outlook, but both of them hope it's a permanent personality change.

Chapter 23
A Fish Tale

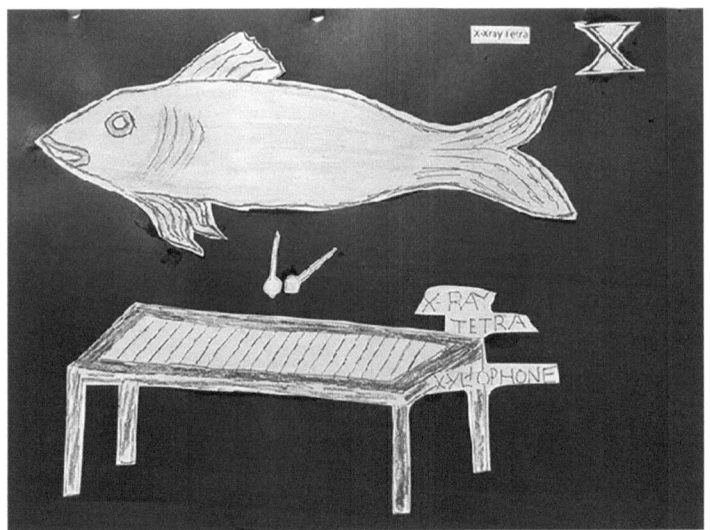

Back in his office, Director Ensemble wastes no time asking about the next student. Quick to respond, Ms. Fermata informs him a student is already set up in the music room and waiting.

"Thanks, I'll go right over."

Secretaries Ms. Fermata and Ms. Treble Clef stand in awe, listening to him. "Did he just say, 'Thank you,' Ms. Treble Clef?"

"I think so, Ms. Fermata."

Both are interested in what has gotten into him.

Walking into the music room, Director Ensemble visualizes a large glass fishbowl on the exhibition table.

Perturbed as well as tired, he promptly returns to the front desk, saying, "What is this? I have no time for your funniness! I'm not laughing!"

Ms. Fermata enters the room, pausing a moment to let Director Ensemble's steam settle. "Sir, this is your next student, X-X-Ray Tetra on xylophone." She politely excuses herself and slips silently out the door.

Alone, Director Ensemble is insecure with this bowl. Stepping to it, he gets a surprise, causing his elk hairs to rise. Residing in the glass bowl, swimming around, is a tritone see-through fish! Starstruck Director Ensemble is unable to take his eyes off this wiggling vertebrate. He watches as the fish swims toward him. Director Ensemble wants to scream but is tongue-tied! He tries again and again to bellow a sound, but nothing escapes his mouth.

A creature emerges from the bowl, taking Director Ensemble by surprise. "Take a video so you can replay as many times as you'd like. Ha! Ha! Got ya! I'm X-X-Ray Tetra. Have no fear, I'll do no harm. I'm C, see-through! Today, for your enjoyment, I'll be playing a short improvisation on my xylophone."

Picking up his mallets, he says, "Oops! Dropped one! Guess my finnitis is acting up!"

X-X-Ray Tetra begins to play, but Director Ensemble interrupts before he gets to measure eight. "Can't you play other than staccato?"

"Well, not exactly, but I have a fantastic reason, sir."

"Oh, I'm sure you do. Is it because you're maestro of the sea?"

"Can I explain, sir? I need to hurry this along. I can't stay out very long, only short intervals at a time, and my time is almost up! Can't you see I'm a fish! My scales are beginning to shrivel and dry. I must return to the water before it's too late. Please excuse me!"

"Is that a fact or fish tale?"

Splash!

"Water everywhere! I'm soaked! Wait until I get my hoofs on you, you slippery … fish!"

The director's face is crimson red with anger written all over it when a voice says, "Don't be mad; it's not good for your BP—you know, blood pressure. Smile! It takes fewer muscles to smile. Plus you'll feel better. I'm X-X-Ray Tetra! Bye!"

Splash! Peeping from the inside of the large glass bowl, X-X-Ray Tetra begins blowing fish-flavored bubbles. Bubbles fill the room. They are seemingly unpopable and last for minutes. Some spell out his name while others remain empty. X-X-Ray Tetra takes the opportunity to rise up one last time and wink at the director.

Splash!

Director Ensemble slams the music room door before X-X-Ray Tetra comes back up for air. However, everyone in the academy hears Director Ensemble say, "This is not real! There's no such thing as a see-through fish! I need a vacation! I'm too old for see-through fishes! Ms. Fermata, where are you?"

The few remaining students and parents are concerned with all the ruckus coming from the music room. Ms. Treble Clef and Ms. Fermata assure them everything is A-OK and Director Ensemble will be with them shortly to conduct the remaining auditions.

Chapter 24
Let's Play, Yak

Tired and worn to a frazzle, Director Ensemble takes a needed break. Going to the kitchen, he fixes his own cup of coffee while his secretaries watch over the front desk. In the back of his mind, he reminiscences about earlier days of the academy, when students were plentiful and finances were stable. He finally realizes that this could be the end of his school, and he must look ahead to the future. What kind of future is yet to be determined, but he decides to keep his chin up and carry on.

The day is not done; soft moonlight is rising in the evening sky. Day three of auditions is ending, and Director Ensemble is plum-tuckered tired. He takes refuge in his office chair. Facing the window, he's lost in the beautiful scenery. His vision is interrupted by the appearance of bubbles containing another message: "Blessed are the pure of heart."

Several times, he reads over the note, letting the words settle in his heart. Again, he asks, "What does this mean? Why are all these bubbles speaking to me?" His concentration is disrupted by Ms. Fermata calling the next student.

Yodel Yak comes forward for her audition. Born in Yosemite National Park, she's spent her life hauling packages up mountains for human folks. Not a graceful job, but traditions hold solid weight in her family.

On the weekends, she's free to work in the local yak spa as an assistant yoga coach. Yaks of all ages gather to exercise, learn, or yatter among the girls, telling tales they couldn't or wouldn't share with their mothers.

Yodel, down to earth, feels no need for the thrills of modern yak life. Her family has followed the same course of tradition to the T. Youngsters know not to try new things outside of their community under threat of being exiled to lower mountains and banned forever from returning.

Unknown to her family and closest friends, Yodel is a yak-yak, a.k.a. one wanting and willing to venture outside beyond family regulations in secrecy. Having a strong desire for more than hauling stuff, Yodel has ambitions and needs purpose in her life. She is drawn to birds singing in the trees and whistling mountain air. Music will be her passage off the mountaintop, giving her a chance to attend Abington Academy. She loves her family but needs this opportunity to nurture the spirit within.

Fearing possible consequences, Yodel keeps her audition a secret. A friend at school has given her free use of an instrument and a place in the band room for storage. The band director, Mrs. Bass, gave permission for her to use a practice room any time one's available. During study hall, Yodel makes haste to the band storage area, gaining access to the yangqin for practice.

The yangqin, known as the Chinese dulcimer, has a total of 144 strings of various thicknesses and is played using bamboo beaters with rubber heads. Trapezoid in shape, the body is made of sandalwood, four or five bridges, and five strings of repeated pitches increasing in volume.

Director Ensemble enters the music room, seeming to be in a rush. He doesn't even bother to sit down before he insists Yodel begin playing. Picking up the bamboo beaters, she begins the G major scale: G-A-B-C-D-E-F#-G-G-F#-E-D-C-B-A-G. Yodel repeats this process several times until the notes are smooth, clear, and without misplacements. She keeps her eyes focused on the music, not on the instrument. Beaters softly held give freedom of movement without letting go.

"That's enough! Go now, and collect a packet from Ms. Fermata or Ms. Treble Clef. Go!"

"Wait! Don't you want my song? I wrote a song just for this audition, sir." "I've heard enough! Save it for later. Go!"

Dismissed, Yodel is disappointed and ready to go home, but the experience fulfilled a lifelong dream of meeting Director Ensemble. Even if she doesn't make the cut, she is happy with the opportunity. She needs to relax from a most stressful time and take a deep breath. "Boy, never wished I was back on the mountain carrying stuff, but this makes the mountain look easy. I'm ready to go back to the mountain."

Only one student remains in the lobby, ending the three-day interview and audition process. A celebration of all applicants, instructors, family, and friends will be held in a few weeks.

Director Ensemble walks out stretching his long elk legs as Zarzuela Zebra waits.

Chapter 25

Zarzuela Zebra

Zarzuela Zebra-Zither

Finally, a voice calls her name. Ms. Fermata escorts Zarzuela down the hall to the music room. Director Ensemble has gone outside to stretch his legs. She has a few minutes to gather her thoughts and prepare her instrument. While waiting for the director, she studies a few of the musical charts on the wall. Fascination takes over, and she is lost within the Circle of Fifths.

Not a musician by trade, Zarzuela is bound and determined to attend Abington. Having chosen the zither, she finds being ambidextrous is definitely a plus. It's five-sided with forty strings that are plucked or strummed. She is able, willing, excited, and ready. "I can master this!"

The word *zither* is German, coming from the Greek *cithara*, giving us the modern guitar. Playing around with her new toy, Zarzuela discovered she was musically inclined, and learning was a breeze. In fact, you could call her an overnight success.

Zarzuela had been spoiled as a child and expects special treatment as a young adult. At the academy, she demands to be introduced differently from the other students and always first. When denied, her sweet, perfect personality changes. Walking over to Ms. Treble Clef, Zarzuela goes into a tantrum. "I'm an A student! I demand to be announced first! My father is the top contributor. Got that?"

Hearing this squabble, Director Ensemble comes rushing over. "Young lady, what is your problem? Where are your manners? Why are you refusing to audition?"

"Don't you know who I am? I don't need to audition! I'm perfect! Who are you to ask such a question?"

"I'm Director Ensemble, and I believe you better settle down, young lady. Maybe it's best you go home and rethink attending. Listen, and abide by all rules, or go, just go. Understand?"

Zarzuela is floored by the manner in which the director is addressing her. Her eyes widen, and briefly, she is speechless.

"But, sir, don't you want the best?" Zarzuela looks at Director Ensemble with her baby-blue eyes, hoping to influence his decision. Apparently, she's never been spoken to in such a way and put in her place. Could this be a future problem?

Director Ensemble watches Zarzuela storm out the door, mad as a zebu. This is the first time she has not gotten her way, and she does not know how to respond. She is at a loss for words and experiencing a heavy heart. Her body is trembling like an earthquake. Outside, the fresh air is so inviting, she prances her way over to the pond. Bubbles catch her attention as they rise from the surface, a few at a time and then way too many to count. The second set has a message: "Blessed are the poor in spirit for theirs is the kingdom of God."

Watching and reading the bubbles, Zarzuela wonders, *Do I have a bad attitude?*

A white dove flies overhead and lands beside her, causing all her black stripes to fall off. Feeling uneasy, she inches her way over to the dove.

"Coo! Coo!"

"What do you want? Shoo, fly, or guess I should say, shoo, dove!" "Coo! Coo!"

"I told you to shoo! Scram!" Silence. "Okay, what is it?" "Zarzuela Zebra."

"How do you know my name?"

"For once in your life, be patient! Follow me back into the academy." "Okay, we're here. Now what?"

"You need to go back and apologize."

"Go back and apologize to those birdbrains? You've got to be kidding." "Watch how you speak, my friend. Remember to be kind."

"I want to go back and apologize to the other students. There, I said it nicely."

The dove remains silent, but Zarzuela knows what she has to do. She takes a deep breath and opens the door to the academy. Going up to the secretaries, Zarzuela speaks so softly both secretaries strain to hear. Ms. Treble Clef says, "Say that again but a little louder."

"I would like to take this opportunity to apologize for my previous behavior."

Zarzuela repeats herself, and this time, Ms. Treble Clef shouts, "Excellent, Zarzuela! We can use our discretion for one worthy student. Congratulations! You're in!"

Ms. Treble Clef and Ms. Fishing Cat are so proud of Zarzuela. They never expected her to return and apologize but were glad to welcome her into the academy. Zarzuela is a special young lady perhaps experiencing a less than loving home. Music introduces her spirit into a world of possibilities.

Chapter 26
Curtain Call

After the last audition, secretaries Ms. Fermata and Ms. Treble Clef are ready to venture down to the Perfect Pitch Café for a relaxed dinner. The last three days of auditions have been tiresome, extremely stressful, and yet a blessing.

The influx of new students has been such a delight. Many will have the experience of a lifetime while at the academy and hopefully will continue their musical studies after graduation.

On their way out the front door, Ms. Treble Clef trips over a large envelope on the stoop. It is addressed to Director Ensemble from Signature Financial and labeled "Urgent." Ms. Fermata scoops it up, asking Ms. Treble Clef, "Should I kick it under a rug or do the right thing and place it on his desk? I'd like to give it a swift kick but think I'll put it where it belongs—on his desk, where he'll find it in the morning."

The two then go down to the café for dinner and great company.

Director Ensemble remains at the academy, sitting behind his large desk in the dark. He knows this is the end of the school he loves dearly, and there is nothing he can do to prevent its demise. Even if he hadn't ignored all those letters and phone calls, he doesn't have the funding to cover the expenses. He rehashes his life, rejoicing over the good times but mainly focusing on the times he has not been kind. Apparently, recent visits from the clownfish and lessons from the bubbles have awakened a part of him from a deep sleep. He decides to go outside for fresh air and to enjoy the full moon.

After dinner, Ms. Treble Clef and Ms. Fermata decide to stop by the academy and find the building pitch-black. Noticing the director's car, they stop to check on him. They find him sitting quietly, staring at the pond. Observing the director, they witness a strange occurrence. Bubbles are frantically rising upward!

"Oh, how awesome! Never in my life have I seen anything like this! What do you make of this, Ms. Treble Clef?"

"I'm clueless. Sure is magical and possibly angelic!"

Bubble struck, all three of them continue watching as the bubbles change colors. Clouds move away so that the moon highlights the late-evening sky, enhancing the shimmer of the bubbles. A message appears:

Blessed are the poor in spirit,
for theirs is the kingdom of heaven.
Blessed are they that mourn,
for they will be comforted.
Blessed are the meek,
for they shall inherit the earth.
Blessed are those who hunger and thirst for
righteousness, for they will be filled.
Blessed are the merciful, for they will be shown mercy.
Blessed are the peacemakers,
for they will be called children of God.
Blessed are you when people insult you, persecute you,
and falsely say all kinds of evil against you because of me.

Director Ensemble is not frightened, nor does he walk back to the academy. Seeking an answer, he asks, "Why are you here?"

A white dove lands on his shoulder. "Do not be afraid. You have been touched by God. He is using you to direct fine young people into the world of music. God is working. He's changing your heart, giving you a new rhythm: peace, love, and joy."

"But, but I'm in trouble! The academy will be closing due to lack of payment. The music will be dead and the walls silent."

Director Ensemble sighs, his brown eyes welling with tears. He knows he hasn't been nice to his secretaries or the students. Without them, the academy wouldn't have survived. Director Ensemble knows he's done wrong. He loves music, the students who make it, and the mountains that echo their songs.

"Do you think God will forgive me?" he asks the dove. "All you have to do is do the right thing."

Director Ensemble turns back toward the academy, resolving to do what is best. Walking back, he thanks his secretaries for all their hard work and dedication. Surprisingly, he gives them two days off and instructs them to assign Kwick Klean, starting this week, as the regular cleanup company. Returning to his office, he also finds the envelope on his desk left by the secretaries. Using his letter opener for its correct purpose, he opens it:

Dear Director Ensemble,

Signature Financial would like to inform you an investor who wants to remain anonymous has paid your delinquent account in full.
He will continue payments if you maintain a positive influence on young musicians in the community sharing your gift of music.

Be blessed.
Marc Lydian, Signature Financial

Director Ensemble struggles to read as tears cloud his vision. He pinches his right hoof to be certain that he is awake and not dreaming. "Who can this investor be that has blessed me?"

Laying the letter aside, he goes outside and gazes at the stars. For the first time in his life, Ensemble feels joy in his heart and can't wait until he can apologize to all he's treated unkindly.

Notes from the Staff:
Glossary of Terms

A440 - tuning standard for musical note A above middle C

Aardvark - animal with a pig-like snout

Aeolian - mode based on the 6th tone in the key of C

Aficionado - person who is very knowledgeable

African Maracas - legend in West Africa tells of the first maracas being made by a goddess who sealed white pebbles in a calabash (bottled gourd)

"Amazing Grace" - hymn written by John Newton a slave trader in 1772

Appalachia - Region in Eastern US from Southern Tier or NY State to northern Alabama to Georgia

Appalachian Dulcimer - string fretted instrument from the zither family having three or four strings dating back to the 1800's originating in the Appalachian Mountains

Appalachian Mountains - system of mountains in Eastern North America

American Arpeggio - notes of a chord played in succession either ascending or descending.

Arrhythmic - out of sync

Ascending - notes flowing upwards

Audition/auditioning - trying out for a position

Bach, J.S-Johann Sebastian - German composer, organist of Baroque Period 1685-1750.

Bagpipes - reed instrument, sweet gentle in tone that normally is in the key of "G"

Bamboo Beaters - raw bamboo sections combined together to play as a musical instrument.

Band Room - section in the school where the music students meet to practice

Banjo - instrument with a long neck, circular body having 4 or 5 strings that is strummed or plucked

Bass - lowest male voice or large musical instrument

Bassoon - woodwind instrument in the double reed family written in bass and tenor clef

Beat - pulse

Beethoven - Ludwig Van, German composer, pianist transition between the Classical and Romantic Eras. 1770-1827

Bow - stick with horsehair stretched along used to play certain instruments

Blessed - fortunate

"Bravo" - exclamation of approval

Buddhist Monks - ordained males and members of the Buddhist community who live a simple and meditative life

Canon in D - by Pachelbel written for three violins and one bass, widely performed

Cello - bowed instrument of the violin family with four strings

Chinese Dulcimer-AKA-Yangqin - trapezoid hammered dulcimer from Iranian Santur or European dulcimer meaning "acclaim."

Chord - sound produced by a group of three or more notes together

Chromatic - notes that do not belong to the scale; half step

Cithara - Ancient Greek & Roman stringed instruments similar to three Lyre in the Lute Family

Clarinet - single reed woodwind instrument played by means of holes and keys Clef=symbol at the end of the staff indicating the pitch of the notes

Clownfish - aquatic creatures that got their name due to their bold coloring (Ding & Dong)

Coda - musical symbol indicating go to the end of the music

Color Guard - team who performs choregraph routines to music

Composer - writer of music

Concerto in C Major - composed by Joseph Hayden and now a staple of the cello repertoire

Crescendo - gradually play louder

Cymbals - percussion instruments consisting of plate-shaped discs made of brass, metal with leather strap

Dance - movement to a musical rhythm

Descending - progression of notes downward

Decrescendo - gradually grow softer

Diminish - make smaller

Djembe - skin covered goblet drum played with bare hands from West Africa.

Dolce - perform with a soft sweet manner

Dominate - fifth degree of a Major or Minor Scale.

Doowop - genre of rhythm and blues originated among African and American youth in the 1940's.

Dulcimer - old instrument box with stretched wire strings across and struck with wooden hammer

Duo - two voice or instruments at the same time

Drum - member of the percussion family and considered the oldest musical instrument

Electronic Tuner - device that detects and displays pitches of musical notes

E Minor Scale - scale relative to G Major: e-f#-g-a-b-c-d-e—e-d-c-b-a-g-f#-e

Ensemble - group of performers.

Entomologist - one who studies insects; branch of Zoology

Etude - musical composition for technical training

Fairy Godmother - female character in fairy tales with magical powers

Fermata - a musical pause

Fiddle - colloquial term for bowed instrument

Fifth Brandenburg Concerto - Bach composition consisting of harpsichord, flute, violin and orchestral accompaniment. Written late 1700's.

Finale - conclusion

Finger Cymbals-AKA-Zills - small metallic cymbals used in belly dancing

Fingerpicks - plastic or metal caps placed on fingertips that brighten the sound

Fine Tuning - small adjustments to achieve the desired pitch

French Horn - coiled brass wind instrument

Free Style Yoga - an approach to yoga that focuses on the strengths of those participating and not the practitioner.

Gibson - guitar manufacturer and other instruments in Kalamazoo, Michigan started by Orville Gibson in 1902

G Major Scale - G-A-B-C-D-E-F#-G G-F#-E-D-C-B-A-G

Gobi Desert - barren plateau of southern Mongolia and northern China

Glissando - to slide

Gong - round percussion instrument also called "Tam Tam" of Chinese origin made of sheet metal

Gourd - trailing or climbing plant that is dried and hollowed

Guitar - stringed instrument that is plucked, strummed and fretted of ancient origin

"Happy Days Are Here Again" - Lyrics written by Milton Ager; lyrics by Jack Yellen. Campaign song for Franklin D. Roosevelt in 1932

Harmonic Minor - basic minor scale pattern with the seventh note raised ½ step

Harmony - pleasing combination of tones in a chord based on thirds

Harp - musical instrument with stretched strings vertically in an open triangular frame and played by plucking

Higuera Tree - AKA fig tree

"How Great Thou Art" - Swedish Hymn written by Carl Gustav Boberg

Hubbub - a busy, noisy situation

Huntington - city in West Virginia located on the Ohio River. Home to the Port of Huntington Tri-State, second-busiest inland port in the US

"I'll Be A Sunbeam" - popular children's hymn composed by Nellie Talbot

I'm In the Mood (Mode) For Love" - written by Jimmy McHugh; Lyrics by Dorothy Fields in 1935

Instrument - any of various devices that produce sound

Ionian - scale composed of natural notes beginning and ending on C

Italian Flute - ½ size flute or piccolo member of the woodwind family

Ivories - white keys of the piano made from ivory. The was banned in the 1950's and the ivory was replaced with plastic

Jazz - music developed in the Southern states in the late 19th Century in New Orleans influenced by the rhythms of West Africa, European Harmony and American singing

Jiaohu - Chinese bowed string instrument

Jig - lively English dance with leaping movements-

Kanawha River - tributary to the Ohio River. 97 miles long in Huntington, WV

Kapella-Capella - sung without music

Kazoo - small American instrument that is blown in and out to produce sound

Key - relation of different chords to each other

"Little Sunbeam" - Written in 1919 by Eben E. Rexford

Lincoln Tunnel - under the Hudson River and 1.5 miles long connecting Weehawken, NJ to West Midtown Manhattan in NYC.

Lullaby" - cradle sung usually sung in 3/4 time

Lyre - Ancient instrument r/t the harp with strings perpendicular to the soundbox

Maestro - the master; initially the title given in Italy to celebrate conductors and teachers

Major - stepwise series of half and whole steps arranged in a particular pattern

Mallet - stick with a rounded end used to strike percussion instrument

Maracas - Latin American instrument made of dried Cuban gourds containing beans

Martin D28 - guitar considered by guitarists as being the classis American guitar

Measure - space between the bar lines in a piece of music

Meerkat - monkey

Melody - organized succession of pitches and notes

Mercy - power to forgive; having compassion

Microphone - amplification system for voice

Minor - scales known as natural, melodic and harmonic with specific patterns

Mixolydian - Mode formed from the fifth note of any Major Scale

Mode - name for each scale using only the white keys

Mother of Pearl-AKA-Nacre - inorganic material produced by some mollusks as an inner shell and used on some musical instruments

Music - written signs that represent vocal or instrumental sound.

Musician - one who performs music

Music Room - or studio where the art of music is played or created

Musically - relates to music

National Bagpipes-AKA - Uilleann Pipes are the characteristic National Bagpipes of Ireland

Natural Trumpet - trumpet that has no means to alter the tones. This type was used during the Civil War to call military to order

Nocturne - piece of music with "night" theme. Invented by Irish composer John Field in the 19th Century

Non-harmonic tone - note not belonging to a certain chord

Note - sound given musical pitch

Numbat - termite eating Australian animal

Oboe - woodwind instrument blown through a double reed

Octave - interval of eight notes

"Old Glory" - nickname for the US Flag

Open G - tuning allowing the G Major chord to be strummed on all six strings: D-G-D-G-B-D

Pachelbel, Johann - German composer, organist of the Baroque Era. 1653-1706. Best known for Canon in D.

"Panis Angelicus" - Latin for "Bread of Angels" written by St. Thomas Aquinas.

"Partita in A Minor" - solo flute by J.S. Bach

Perfect Pitch-AKA-absolute pitch - retaining the sound. Rare ability to identify musical note without a reference note

Percussion - striking of one body against another-

Perfect Fifth - musical interval corresponding to two pitches

Perfect Pitch-AKA-absolute pitch - is a rare ability to recreate a musical tone without a reference note

Performance - act of presenting

Phrase - a musical sentence usually 4-8 bars

Piano - modern keyboard

Pick - a piece of flat plastic held between thumb and middle finger used to strum

Picking - using a pick in order to strike the strings

Pluck - pull quick on the string with your finger or plectrum

Plucked - see above

Prelude - introductory piece of the music.

Prodigy - person with extraordinary talent or ability

Putnum County - One of the fifty counties admitted to the union to what is now known as WV

Qichak - Ancient Iranian instrument

Quintet - group of five instruments or singers

Rain sticks - long hollow tubes filled with beans when turned sound like rain

Red House Shoal - rock ledge in the Kanawha River with a three foot drop

Rehearsal - musical practice

Repeat Sign - indicates a section in the music should be repeated

Resonates - resounding

Rhythmic - relates to time, beat or meter.

Ringtones - customized sound.

Rhythm - movement by regular recurrence of beat.

Rock 'n Roll - music that originates in the mid-50's included gospel, jump blues, boogie woogie, rhythm & blues and country

Rosin - wax type substance used on bows to make them adhere to the strings to produce sound

Santur - string instrument from Iran in the Zither Family

Scale - sequence of notes in ascending and descending order

Sheep Gut - natural fiber found in the intestines in animals used in instruments

Shilly-shallied - to show hesitation

Shirley Temple - American actress

Shoal - natural submerged ridge

Signature - musical notation specifying how many beats per measure

Sing - act of producing sounds with voice using tone, rhythm and vocal technique

Sixteenth Note - played ½ duration of the eighth note

Six-eight time - six eight notes per bar of music

Sixty-fourth note - note played half the duration of the thirty-second

Sloth - mammal of South and Central America know for slowness and hanging upside down

Solo - performance by one

Song Stuck Syndrome - sometimes referred to as brain worm-catchy piece of music that won't leave your mind

Sound - particular auditory impression; tone

Soundboard - wooden sheet, usually spruce that can enhance the tone of an instrument

Staccato - playing a note sharp and less than it's value

Step - interval between one degree and the next

Strum - sweep across the strings with finger or plectrum to make sound

Symphony - large gathering of musicians performing a musical composition with 3-4 movements

Syncopated - displaced beats or accents so that the strong=weak and vice versa

Tchaikovsky - Russian composer of the Romantic Period. Famous for "The Nutcracker" and "Sleeping Beauty"

Temple, Shirley - American actress who began acting at an early age of 6 becoming one of Hollywood's biggest actresses

Tempo - speed of the music

Tibetan Singing Bowl - type of bell that vibrates and produces a rich, deep tone. AKA singing bowl. Promotes relaxation and healing

Timbre - quality of musical sound

Tone - musical or vocal sound referring to pitch, quality or strength

Tooth Fairy - fantasy character that visits young children at night bringing a gift for loosing a tooth

Toy Trumpet - play instrument

Treble Clef - musical symbol indicating the pitch of written notes

Triad - group of three notes

Triple Notes or triplet - rhythm of three notes played in space of two

Tuba - droplet shaped and lowest pitched musical instrument in the brass family

Tune - to bring the pitch of an instrument up to A440

Tunning Pegs - wooden piece or other type of material that is turned to tighten or loosen a string to bring the pitch to A440

Two-Part Harmony - more than one note played together and produce pleasing sound

Uakari - New World monkey

Uilleann Pipes - Irish Bagpipes played by wind supplied by bellows held under the arms

Unison - all voices singing the same pitch

Union Pipes - earlier name for the Uillean Pipes

Upbeat - weak beat that comes before the strong of a measure

Venus Fly Trap - perennial carnivorous plant that catches and digests insects

Vervet - small black faced monkey common in East Africa

Viola - an alto instrument of the string family

Violin - sometimes called a fiddle; wooden stringed instrument with a very high pitch and played with a bow

Voice-voice - refers to instrument parts as well as the singing voice

Vivaldi, Antonia - Italian composer, violinist, priest

Wallaby - small to medium mammal similar to a kangaroo

Waltz - dance in triple time

Washboard - percussion instrument with a ribbed metal surface played with spoons or fingerpicks

"Waltz of the Flowers" - second act of "The Nutcracker" by Tchaikovsky

X-Xray Tetra - translucent fish found in the Amazon basin

Xylophone - percussion instrument consisting of graduated wooden bars played by soft or hard hammers

Yak - domesticated oxen used in Tibet to carry goods along the mountains

Yangqin - Chinese hammered dulcimer

Yodel - form of singing

Yoga Tree - approach to yoga that draws on inner resources of the practitioner

Yosemite National Park - located in California known for the ancient sequoia trees, magnificent views and towering waterfalls.

Zarzuela - Spanish lyric part spoken and sung musical

Zebu - ox

Zither - musical instrument with numerous strings stretched across the flat wooden sound box

Lyrical
Bibliography

Neufeldt, Victoria
Webster's New World Dictionary ©1990, 1995
ISBN 0-671-51982-4

Whitfield, Jane Shaw
Webster's New World Crossword Puzzle Dictionary
Second Edition ©1997
ISBN 978-1-328-71031-4

Jellis,Susan
Microsoft Encarta Thesaurus
ISBN 0-312-98363-8

Merriam-Webster, Inc.
The Merriam-Webster Thesaurus
ISBN 978-0-87779-850-7

Schaffer, Edy Garcia
The New Comprehensive A-Z Crossword Dictionary ©1995
ISBN 13: 978-0-380-7242253
    10: 0-380-72425-1

Publications, Mel Bay
Encyclopedia of Scales, Modes and Melodic Patterns ©1997

MacArthur, John
The MacArthur Study Bible ©1997
New King James Version

www.google.com
www.wikipedia.com
Hymnary.org